Gathering Boards

Gathering Boards

Seasonal *Cheese* and *Charcuterie* Spreads for Easy and Memorable Entertaining

SARAH ZIMMERMAN TUTHILL

Globe
Pequot

Essex, Connecticut

Globe
Pequot

An imprint of Globe Pequot, the trade division of
The Rowman & Littlefield Publishing Group, Inc.
4501 Forbes Blvd., Ste. 200
Lanham, MD 20706
www.rowman.com

Distributed by NATIONAL BOOK NETWORK

British Library Cataloguing in Publication Information available

Library of Congress Cataloging-in-Publication Data
Names: Tuthill, Sarah Zimmerman, author.
Title: Gathering boards : seasonal cheese and charcuterie spreads for easy
    and memorable entertaining / Sarah Zimmerman Tuthill.
Description: Essex, Connecticut : Globe Pequot, [2024]
Identifiers: LCCN 2023041980 (print) | LCCN 2023041981 (ebook) | ISBN
    9781493075553 (cloth) | ISBN 9781493075560 (epub)
Subjects: LCSH: Appetizers. | Cheese—Varieties. | Food presentation. | Snack
    foods. | LCGFT: Cookbooks.
Classification: LCC TX382 .T87 2024 (print) | LCC TX382 (ebook) | DDC
    641.81/173—dc23/eng/20230927
LC record available at https://lccn.loc.gov/2023041980
LC ebook record available at https://lccn.loc.gov/2023041981

♾™ The paper used in this publication meets the minimum requirements of
American National Standard for Information Sciences—Permanence of Paper
for Printed Library Materials, ANSI/NISO Z39.48-1992.

For my girls
In memory of my Mom
ILYMTTCT

Contents

Introduction

IT WAS TEN MINUTES BEFORE GUESTS WERE TO ARRIVE and I was frantically digging for little glass bowls to place nuts on various tables, just as my mother had taught me. "It's not cocktail hour without a bowl of nuts," she would say. With appetizers in the oven and dinner simmering on the stove, I gave up the search and instead poured the way-too-large bags of almonds, cashews, and peanuts I'd bought into three rustic salad bowls and stuck them, along with an even bigger bowl of olives, on the entry table next to candles and a flower arrangement.

I can't recall what I served for dinner that night, but what I do remember is the number of compliments I got on the "beautiful buffet of nuts and olives." Really? That's what impressed my friends?

That was the last time I cooked a formal meal for a crowd, but also when I fell in love with entertaining. The truth is, you don't have to be a culinary genius to throw a good party. In fact, you don't have to know how to cook at all. By merely presenting food and drinks in an inventive, beautiful, or whimsical way, you can turn the ordinary into the extraordinary.

As a corporate communications professional, writer, and single mom, this revelation changed my entertaining game for good. My mantra became "Keep it simple but make it memorable."

I started focusing on how to *display* food rather than prepare it, amassing a collection of wooden boards and bowls, along with unusual objects like a framed mirror or rustic step stool. I searched for anything on which to uniquely present uncomplicated, store-bought ingredients like wedges of artisanal cheeses, swaths of salty charcuterie meats, bounteous baskets of breads, and, of course, big bowls of nuts and olives.

One of my more unconventional finds is an antique shirtsleeve ironing board, long and thin and perfect for a row of crackers or salami. And there's the primitive wooden tool caddy that I use to hold candles, flowers, or jars of nuts and olives. Even an old tackle box can find new life as a playful way to serve snacks.

Before long, my friends and family came to expect an inventive spread for any get-together, from book clubs to holiday parties. And when cooking was compulsory, like for Thanksgiving, my only other job was to make the table look pretty. "I can do that," I would say. "That's easy."

And thus, the concept of EZPZ Gatherings was born.

As my daughters, Lydia and Edie, grew older I started asking myself what the next chapter in my life might look like. I'd been freelance writing about food and restaurants for years, but wanted to get my hands dirty, to create and build something. Not intent on offering full-service catering, I had what back then was a novel idea: a cheese and charcuterie service that focuses solely on creating "Gathering Boards"—impressive appetizer spreads for gatherings of all sizes.

Today, I run EZPZ Gatherings out of a sunny storefront just blocks from my home in Aspinwall, a quaint suburb of Pittsburgh, Pennsylvania. It's both a commercial kitchen and a space for customers to join my "Boarding School" workshops to learn the art of cheese and charcuterie styling. In this book, I'll teach you those skills, and a whole lot more.

Here you'll get not only the tricks of the cheese-and-charcuterie styling trade, but also presentation concepts, festive drink pairings, and décor inspiration for every season. *Gathering Boards* is not your typical cookbook, nor is it filled with hard-to-find ingredients and precise measurements. Think of it as a collection of inspiring images and easy-to-follow ideas that can be mixed, matched, and made your own. This is your year-round guide for simple yet memorable gatherings.

Cheers!

Sarah

GATHERING BOARDS

How to Get the Most Out of Gathering Boards

GATHERING BOARDS ISN'T A TYPICAL COOKBOOK filled with recipes using hard-to-find ingredients or precise measurements. Instead, think of it as a collection of inspiring images and easy-to-follow ideas that can be mixed, matched, and made your own.

In the first section, you'll find what you need to get started making your own impressive spreads. It's chock-full of information on how to choose your cheeses, meats, and other ingredients and how to create balance on your boards. You'll learn about choosing a platter and other utensils, as well as tips on prepping, arranging, and storing your ingredients.

The next four sections make up a year-round guide for simple yet memorable entertaining. For each season, you'll find an array of boards fit for specific celebrations, along with my own stories that inspired them. You'll not only learn how to create your own version of these special boards, but also discover the tricks of the cheese and charcuterie trade, with food-styling tips that will wow even the most discerning of your foodie friends. Beyond the food, I share loads of additional entertaining tips like drink pairings and uncomplicated DIY décor projects to make your gatherings memorable.

In addition to appetizer boards styled for specific holidays and occasions, you will also discover spreads designed for everyday use—like easy meals and fun desserts that, when thoughtfully displayed on a large board or platter, seem to magically bring everyone to the table.

Throughout this book, quantities and ingredients are unspecific by design, meant to inspire but also encourage you to experiment with your own combinations and components. Yet, though this book is more about arranging food than cooking it, the final section is a collection of some of my go-to recipes—those that are mentioned in stories about my family and friends, that hold special memories.

Board Basics

"EVERYTHING IS BETTER ON A BOARD." I coined this adage long before making a career of it. My two girls would come home from grade school ravenous, toss open the pantry, and complain, "We have nothing to eat," before grabbing whatever snacks they could get their hands on, leaving a stream of crumbs in their wakes. At some point I wised up and would set out a tray of pretzels and hummus, or cheese and crackers, or a bowl loaded up with fruit. "Wow, you got new snacks!" they'd exclaim, despite it being the exact same food they'd just turned their nose up to.

This idea that everything tastes better if it's displayed on a platter or board holds true for kids and adults alike. I guess it's the same reason buffets are so popular—people like to see their options and make their own choices. Plus, there's nothing like the "make your own" component that gets guests excited about the food you're serving. Over the years, I've done them all: taco boards and hot dog boards for dinner, pancake boards and bagel boards for breakfast, sandwich boards and salad boards for lunch.

My favorite, of course, are appetizer boards, and specifically meats and cheeses. I veer off the traditional path to include some spin-offs in the shop, at home, and in this book, but my first love will always be a bountiful board filled with cheese and charcuterie.

Choosing Your Cheese

I LIVED IN SWITZERLAND FOR A YEAR and spent a lot of time wandering into local *Käserei*, tasting Swiss Gruyères, Emmentals, and local mountain Käse. I also had more than my fair share of fondue and raclette, two cheesy dishes for which the country is known. But it wasn't until I moved back home to Pittsburgh that I truly fell in love with cheese.

On any given weekend, just about every foodie, home cook, and chef makes a Saturday morning pilgrimage to the city's Strip District—a historic shopping district lined with meat and fish markets, ethnic grocers, produce stands, and an assortment of sidewalk vendors. My first stop is always the cheese counter at Pennsylvania Macaroni Company, or "Penn Mac" to locals.

Depending on the timing, the line could be fifty people deep, but it's always worth the wait—especially if your number was called by the beloved cheese

monger affectionately known as Dear Heart. "What d'ya need, dear heart?" she'd holler from behind the counter, always friendly yet efficient. I'd tell her I'm doing a cheese board for ten, and within seconds I'd be tasting a chunk of salty Parmigiano Reggiano or a sliver of nutty aged Gouda. "OK, dear heart, so you'll need three cheeses," she'd insist, handing me a shmear of tangy Maytag blue. "Let's make sure you have a variety of taste and texture. Oh, and this one will add some nice color," she'd say, sliding a bright orange chard of aged cheddar across the counter.

I never turned down her suggestions, and not once was I disappointed with the combinations she created for me and my guests. She has long since retired, but I still hear her voice in my head every time I'm standing at the cheese counter.

Cheese classifications abound and can be studied at length. Here are the most common ways cheese makers, mongers, and aficionados categorize it.

Classification by Texture

A cheese's texture, which ranges from soft to hard, is determined by its firmness. Simply put, the lower the moisture content, the firmer the cheese. Every cheese falls into one of four categories: hard, semi-hard, soft, and fresh.

	CHARACTERISTICS	EXAMPLES
HARD	Crumbly, easy to grate, gritty	Parmesan, Romano
SEMI-HARD	Smooth, easy to slice or shred	Cheddar, Swiss, Manchego
SOFT	Creamy, spreadable	Camembert, Brie
FRESH	Soft, stretchy, grainy, or crumbly	Cottage, ricotta

Classification by Covering

Cheeses can also be differentiated by their covering, or type or rind. Cloth, bark, and, most commonly, wax might be wrapped around cheese to preserve it, but you should avoid eating those. Three other types of rinds form organically and are meant to be eaten for their flavor and texture. Some spreadable and fresh cheeses don't have rinds at all. Every cheese falls into one of six categories: waxed, bloomy, natural, washed, blue, and fresh.

	PROCESS	CHARACTERISTICS	EXAMPLES
WAXED	Pressed cheeses dipped and sealed in wax before aging	Range from semi-hard and meltable to dense and crumbly	Gouda, Edam
BLOOMY	Mold added to milk or sprayed on before aging	Funky, tangy, or mild; soft or semi-soft	Brie, Camembert
NATURAL	No covering, little intervention during aging process	Rustic exterior, earthy cave-like flavor	Cheddar, Parmesan, Manchego
WASHED	Bathed, rubbed, or sprayed with brine or alcohol continuously as it ripens	Orange or reddish hue, so-called "stinky" cheeses	Muenster, feta
BLUE	Cultured with bacteria that is sprayed before aging	Blue/green veins, pungent, salty	Stilton, Roquefort, Gorgonzola
FRESH	Unripened, un-aged, made from fresh curds	High water content; grainy, stretchy, or creamy	Cottage, ricotta, mozzarella

Classification by Animal Source

Milk is the main ingredient of any cheese, so the animal from which it comes impacts its flavor and texture. The animal's breed, geographical location, and diet affect the levels of water, lactose, lipids, and proteins found in cheese. The most popular cheeses fall into four categories: cow, goat, sheep, and buffalo.

	CHARACTERISTICS	EXAMPLES
COW	Most commonly used dairy, relatively high-fat content, neutral and mild flavors	Cheddar, Swiss, Parmesan, Gouda, Camembert
GOAT	Higher in fat and minerals, less lactose, softer, tangy flavor	Chèvre, Humboldt Fog
SHEEP	Higher in fat than goat or cow, grassy and nutty flavors	Manchego, Roquefort, pecorino
BUFFALO	High fat content, smooth and white, sweet and acidic flavors	Buffalo mozzarella, burrata, stracciatella

The Bottom Line

Cheese and its various classifications can be overwhelming and stressful, especially when you get to the front of the line at the cheese counter and still don't know what to order. Armed with all this information, you might be tempted to come home with a dozen packages of cheese! Once you've gotten the gist, you'll find some favorites and should be able to limit your choices to three to five to create a cheese board with just the right balance of what I consider to be the three most important characteristics:

CONSISTENCY: Choose something firm and easy to slice, like cheddar and Manchego. Next, find a hard cheese such as a Parmesan, the kind that often breaks off into shards or chunks and can have a granular texture. Lastly, add a soft and spreadable cheese, like Brie or goat cheese.

Aged Gouda, Brie, and Manchego (l–r)
make a beautiful and delicious trio
from which to build a cheese board.

TASTE: For a successful board, avoid cheeses that are one note. Instead of all super mild or all rich and funky, you want to hit up all your taste buds and ensure that there's enough variety to accommodate your guests' varying preferences. I always include something with wide appeal, like a buttery Havarti, mild cheddar, or Monterey Jack. To counter that, pick a cheese with a stronger flavor like a sharp cheddar or Asiago, a nutty aged Manchego, or an unguent Parmesan. Round it out with a tangy goat cheese or feta and a pungent blue cheese.

COLOR: A cheese's color is primarily impacted by animal breed, aging, and the use of natural additives. Cheese, as we know, is typically a shade of orange, yellow, or white, so for visual appeal, I like to include a variety of colors, as well as something with a unique or seasonal shade. A vibrant green English Derby infused with sage, for example, produces a gorgeous green marbling effect, or a blueberry goat cheese brings a beautiful shade of purple.

When people ask what my favorite cheese is, I always say it's like asking which child I love most. But if forced to choose, I'd say my ideal cheese board always includes a creamy Brie, a nutty Manchego, and a well-aged sharp cheddar. Start there and you can't go wrong. I think Dear Heart would approve.

Charcuterie 101

WHILE IT MAY SEEM LIKE *CHARCUTERIE* is a new and often amusingly mispronounced concept fashioned by TikTok and Instagram influencers, its history reaches back to fifteenth-century France. Charcuterie (shar-KOO-ta-REE) is a specific term referring to specialty cured meats made from pork. Today's charcuterie often includes pork, but the definition has loosened to reflect other meats served in cultures around the world.

And thanks to social media, Americans have really relaxed the use of the term *charcuterie*, using it to describe just about any food you can put on a board. Call me a stickler, but you won't see me slapping candy and cookies on a wooden board and calling it "dessert charcuterie." In fact, I'm such a traditionalist (or nerd) that you'll hear me say "cheese *and* charcuterie board" because, technically, a charcuterie board is only a selection of meats.

In broad terms, charcuterie encompasses all types of cured meats, fresh and smoked sausages, and spreadable preparations and falls into three categories: whole muscle, coarse ground, and fine ground.

	CHARACTERISTICS	EXAMPLES
WHOLE-MUSCLE CHARCUTERIE	Made from whole cuts of meat that are cured, smoked, and aged. Meat is salted and spiced before being aged for weeks or months.	Bresaola, prosciutto, pancetta
COARSE-GROUND CHARCUTERIE	Made from coarsely ground meats that are blended with spices and other ingredients. The meat is stuffed into casings to be cured, then hung to dry and age for weeks to months.	Salami, chorizo, summer sausage
FINE-GROUND CHARCUTERIE	Made from finely ground meat that is emulsified with fat and other ingredients before being stuffed into casings and cooked. The meat is typically cooked in a water bath or oven, then cooled and refrigerated until it is ready to be served.	Pâté, terrine, rillettes

For the boards in this book, I focus on the most popular charcuterie that you can find in just about any grocery store or market. Here are a few of my favorites:

GENOA SALAMI: Slightly spicy and smoky, this crowd-pleaser is made from pork and seasoned with wine, garlic, salt, and peppercorns. The ingredients are ground and stuffed sausage-style into a casing. Genoa salami is then fermented to preserve its tangy flavor.

Some of the most popular charcuterie meats include (l–r) Genoa salami, hard salami, capocollo, and prosciutto.

HARD SALAMI: As its name suggests, hard salami is firmer and denser than Genoa because it contains less moisture. Using pork, garlic, and other seasonings, it is cured, air-dried, and wrapped in a casing and can be enjoyed sliced a bit thick.

PROSCIUTTO: This delicacy is made by aging and dehydrating the hind leg or thigh of a pig or boar through a complex process of salting, hanging, pressing, and cleaning that can last up to a couple of years. The result is a subtly sweet and salty charcuterie best served sliced paper thin.

CAPOCOLLO: This is a whole-muscle, aged, and cured pork product (as opposed to the sausage-like preparation of salami). Also called coppa or capacolla, depending on the region, it's deep red in color with white marbles of fat and is best served sliced thin.

Rounding It Out

CHEESE AND MEATS MAY BE THE STAR, but when it comes to creating a show-stopping board, the supporting characters make for rave reviews. Seasonal fruits, vegetables, and fresh herbs bring a board to life, while dips and spreads give guests unlimited pairing possibilities. Nuts and seeds provide a sweet and savory crunch, and a good selection of breads and crackers is a must. The choices are infinite, so start with some of your favorites, or choose from some of mine:

SOMETHING FRESH: Although most fruits and vegetables can be found year-round at a supermarket, I like to highlight seasonal produce to keep boards feeling fresh. Grapes are the quintessential accompaniment for cheese and charcuterie, but berries are also a great choice to add color and flavor. Thin slices of citrus fruits like lemons and oranges make for a lovely presentation, too, and can be dried for a more rustic look. Though others in the biz opt not to include vegetables on their boards, I love the brightness they add. Gorgeous pink radishes, green snap peas, and rainbow carrots are a light alternative to crackers for soft herbed cheeses.

Herbs and edible flowers also bring a board to life. In the spring and summer, the window box outside my shop is an abundant source. Rosemary is my signature, featured on most of my boards and on my logo (shout out to my talented niece who created it!). I also grow dill, parsley, sage, and thyme but when winter comes, I use store-bought herbs and locally sourced microgreens to give boards that fresh touch.

SOMETHING SALTY: Brine is a solution of salt in water that can be used to preserve and add flavor to almost any vegetable or fruit—it is what makes a cucumber a pickle, for example. Adding a variety of pickles and olives is the perfect foil for all the rich meats and cheeses. In addition to cucumbers, try using other pickled veggies like green beans, asparagus, or peppers, most of which can be readily found at grocery stores or farmers' markets.

SOMETHING SPREADABLE: At the shop, we include seasonal spreads and love using local honeys and jams. Just about any cheese is enhanced when drizzled with honey, from blue to cheddar. One of my favorite pairings is honey mixed in or just drizzled on top of goat cheese. I often place a generous piece of luscious honeycomb right on top of a soft, creamy Brie. Likewise, you cannot go wrong by adding jam or fruit spread to a cheese and charcuterie

board. I love trying small-batch jam makers who create unique flavor profiles that add an interesting twist to our boards. A generous dab of rich fig jam on top of a log of goat cheese is delicious on a slice of baguette. Topping fresh ricotta with a blueberry-lemon jam is another treat for the taste buds. Try finding locally made spreads at your local market and have fun experimenting!

SOMETHING CRUNCHY, SOMETHING CHEWY: As you make your way through a rich cheese and charcuterie board, you start looking for a bit of crunch or chew. That is why nuts, seeds, and dried fruit are a great addition and provide a much-needed break for your taste buds. Almonds are good with most any cheese or meat, and the sweet Spanish Marconas are my favorite. Up there on my list are candied nuts, like pecans or walnuts. For some chewiness, dried fruits like apricots, figs, and cranberries are an important element to pair with the rest of the board.

SOMETHING CARBY: I'm a carb girl and proud of it! But at EZPZ, we don't typically include bread and crackers on our boards for a couple of reasons. First, they take up valuable real estate on a platter that can otherwise be filled with more of the good stuff. And if the board will be placed in a refrigerator before serving, you don't want your crackers to get soggy. Served on the side, my favorites include a sliced baguette, a crunchy water cracker, and a chewy crisp with seeds and dried fruit. As always, variety is key.

Add crunch and salt to your boards with items like olives and nuts.

Choosing a Board

MY MOM LOVED PIGS, an obsession that started when she took my sister and me to see *Charlotte's Web* in 1973. She fell in love with Wilbur and over the years amassed a collection of pig figurines, ornaments, paintings, mugs, and pillows. Once, I asked my kids to count all the pigs they could find in my parents' house, and they tired of the game after finding more than one hundred of them. Among my favorite pigs is a wooden tray, likely an antique trivet, that she used to serve cheese and crackers.

That one stays at my parents' house, but I've since found a few similar piggy boards that are now among an extensive collection of platters, baskets, and trays that line the walls of my shop. Some are antique, some are not. Some are basic, while others are found items I've repurposed for serving. They are also a part of the inventory I use for EZPZ customers who love their character and uniqueness (and are often disappointed when they have to return them).

Whether you have a collection of your own or are looking to purchase a platter for an upcoming gathering, choosing the right one is the first step to making a successful presentation. Think about the vibe and ambiance of your party, as well as accompanying decorations and a theme. No matter what you choose, be sure it is safe and nonporous or add food-safe paper liners to protect it and your guests. Here are some materials to fit any mood and style:

RUSTIC: If you are going for casual and neutral, look for natural materials that will bring warmth to the table.

- Wooden boards and bowls
- Woven baskets and trays
- Slate and marble slabs

MODERN: Clean and minimalist, these materials complement any type of food and décor and are a clean and sleek addition to the table.

- Clear acrylic
- Molded or cast aluminum
- Colorful melamine
- Eco-chic recycled bamboo

Some of the vast collection of boards
I have on display in my shop.

VINTAGE: Whether you call it granny-chic or antique, vintage platters, plates, and trays infuse a table with charm and personality.

- Delicately patterned porcelain/china

- Sturdy stoneware

- Ornate silver, silver plate, copper, or brass

- Kitschy metal snack trays

Knife Selection

ONCE YOU'VE CHOSEN JUST THE RIGHT BOARD to display your meats and cheeses, next up is serving and slicing utensils. Regardless of which knife you choose, make sure it's sharp and well-maintained to ensure clean, precise cuts. There are several types of cheese and charcuterie knives, each one designed for a specific type. Ultimately the knives you choose will depend on your personal preference for cutting and serving.

Cheese Knives

CHEESE PLANE: This is a flat, thin blade with a sharp edge that is used to slice thin, even pieces of cheese.

CHEESE CLEAVER: This is a heavy, rectangular blade with a sharp edge that is used to cut hard and crumbly cheeses like cheddar or Gouda.

CHEESE FORK: This is a fork-like tool with two prongs that is used to hold and cut soft or crumbly cheeses like feta or goat cheese.

PARMESAN KNIFE: This is a small, sharp knife with a pointed tip that is used to cut hard and aged cheeses like Parmesan.

SPREADER KNIFE: This is a short, wide knife with a blunt edge that is used to spread soft cheeses like Brie or Camembert.

SOFT CHEESE KNIFE: This is a knife with holes in the blade that prevent soft cheeses from sticking to the blade while cutting.

WIRE CHEESE SLICER: This is a tool with a wire blade that is used to slice very thin, even pieces of cheese.

Charcuterie Knives

CHEF'S KNIFE: A chef's knife can also work well for cutting charcuterie. This versatile knife has a wide blade that can be used for a variety of cutting tasks, including slicing through meats and cheeses.

SLICING KNIFE: A slicing knife is a long, thin knife with a sharp, narrow blade that is perfect for cutting thin slices of charcuterie. Look for a knife with a blade that is at least nine inches long and that has a comfortable handle for easy slicing.

PARING KNIFE: A paring knife is a small, lightweight knife with a thin blade that can be used for more-precise cutting tasks. This knife can be helpful for cutting small pieces of charcuterie or for trimming off any unwanted fat or rind.

CLEAVER: If you're dealing with larger pieces of charcuterie, like a whole ham or salami, a cleaver can be a good choice. This heavy-duty knife has a thick blade that can power through dense meats and bones.

Serving Sizes

GATHERING BOARDS IS ALL ABOUT INSPIRING CREATIVITY, which is why you won't find hard-to-follow recipes or precise measurements. While you don't want your guests to starve, you also don't want any of your delicious, and often pricey, food to go to waste. When preparing your boards, start with the following serving suggestions, keeping in mind your guests' appetites and preferences, other food you are serving, and how long your event will last.

CHEESE: 2 ounces per person

VEGGIES: 6 ounces per person

MEAT: 2 ounces per person

FRUITS: 6 ounces per person

NUTS: 3 tablespoons per person

HUMMUS/DIP: ½ cup per person

BREAD/CRACKERS: 5 ounces per person

Example: If you are having ten guests and are serving four cheeses, you will want to get about 5 ounces of each type of cheese: 10 guests × 2 ounces = 20 ounces (5 ounces each).

Prepping, Arranging, and Storing

Tips for Prepping a Gathering Board

- Get everything out on the counter to assess what you're going to put on your board. This is a good time to check that you have that essential balance of taste, texture, and color, as well as to gauge what size board or platter you will need.

- Slicing the meat and breaking down large wedges of cheese into small servings is essential for a successful board. Aside from being more sanitary, bite-size pieces are just easier to eat. Guests tend to avoid larger, unsliced items and go for the ones that are easy to grab.

- Slice the soft cheeses like Brie and goat cheese logs first, when they are nice and cold. If they get too warm, throw them back in the refrigerator for twenty minutes, or in the freezer for about ten minutes, to firm up.

- It's just the opposite for semi-hard cheeses like cheddar and Manchego. Slice these after they have sat out for about ten to twenty minutes. This ensures they don't crumble or crack while you are slicing.

- Handle thin and delicate charcuterie, like capocollo and prosciutto, when it is cold so it doesn't stick together or tear easily.

- If you are going to fold or roll a thicker sliced charcuterie like salami, let it sit out for about ten to twenty minutes. If it's too cold, the folds will open right back up.

Steps for Arranging a Gathering Board

Now that you've got everything prepared, it's time to begin arranging. While there are detailed styling tricks in the chapters that follow, these are some general tips to get started:

1. Start by laying down food-safe paper on your board if needed. Place any bowls for nuts or olives, as well as jars of jam or honey, if you are serving them. This can be done ahead of time.

2. Next, begin placing the various cheeses on the board. Arrange some in precise rows using rectangular, square, and triangle-shaped slices. These can be straight lines or ones that curve to create some visual interest. For cubed or crumbled cheese, stack them in neat but casual piles. If the board is large, consider at least two rows or stacks of every cheese—one on each end of the board.

3. Next, arrange the meats. Again, I prefer having some in neat rows, others rolled or folded, along with piles or stacks of thicker hard salami. While there is nothing wrong with a simple row of sliced meats, varying techniques draw guests into the board and create some visual interest.

4. Fill in the gaps with fresh and dried fruits. This is a good time to add pops of color throughout the board. You can also guide guests toward delicious pairings by placing fruits like, for example, strawberries near the Brie or dried apricots with Manchego—both classic combinations.

5. Pour the nuts and olives into the bowls or create piles directly on the board to fill any empty space. For briny additions like pickles and olives, be sure not to place them next to items that may get soggy from their juices.

6. Tuck fresh herbs between cheese slices and lay them atop a row of salami. Fresh herbs give the final touch—like a ribbon on a wrapped package.

7. If there's room, feel free to add crackers and breads to the board. I often serve them separately in a basket or bowl.

Tips on Serving Temperatures

- Cheese and charcuterie are best served at room temperature. If you store them in the refrigerator, remove at least twenty minutes prior to guests arriving to allow their complex flavors to shine.

- For cheese, four hours is the maximum it should be left out of the refrigerator. Not only will it start to dry out, but bacteria will form if left out too long, creating the potential to cause sickness.

- Cured charcuterie can typically sit out for up to two hours before bacteria can begin to form.

- If it's a particularly warm day, don't let your board sit out longer than an hour to avoid the risk of spoilage.

Tips on Storing Meat and Cheese

- If you'd like to prepare your board a few hours in advance, wrap it in plastic and place in the refrigerator. Be sure to leave out the crackers, nuts, or other items that have the potential to get soggy.

- You can slice and prep a day or two in advance, then store sliced meats and cheeses in the refrigerator until you are ready to assemble your board. Be sure to wrap each separately so as not to combine flavors.

- For both meat and cheese, a resealable plastic bag will do the trick, but the ideal way to store them is to first wrap them in wax, parchment, or cheese paper. For hard cheeses, consider leaving the plastic bag open to allow the cheese to breathe.

Winter Gathering Boards

MOST PEOPLE SEEM TO HAVE A FAVORITE SEASON, but I don't know many who choose winter. Depending on where you live, the weather can be cold, wet, and unpredictable, making it the most challenging time to stay motivated, productive, and connected.

When days grow short and the temperatures begin to drop, our human instinct is to hunker down. But as much as I lament the increased darkness—the sun sets as early as 4:00 p.m. where I'm from—I try to take advantage of longer evenings by reading more and, let's be honest, adding more shows to my watch list, which I binge without guilt. And yet, as an extrovert, what I miss this time of year is some social interaction.

Indeed, winter makes getting together a bit more difficult, but the season is also home to some of the most celebrated holidays, like Christmas, Hanukkah, and Kwanzaa, that provide meaningful incentive to come together with friends and family. Add New Year's Eve and Valentine's Day to the mix, and you've got plenty to celebrate in the dead of winter, whether it's a lively holiday party or a cozy night by the fire.

Holiday Cheese and Charcuterie Wreath

THE HOLIDAYS CAN BE A TRICKY TIME FOR FAMILIES of all shapes and sizes. As a divorced parent, I am proud that my "wasband" DeWayne and I don't just co-parent well but have continued to spend just about every holiday together as one big happy family. I like to say we put the fun in dysfunctional!

Christmas in particular is very meaningful to our extended family. You see, long before he and I were married, my mom and his mom were very close friends, part of a group of women we started to call the "Church Ladies," a term coined by the popular *Saturday Night Live* skit. Yes, they all met at church, but their true bonds grew beyond it and often over several glasses of chardonnay. Together, the Church Lady families celebrated holidays big and small, each taking on a different holiday.

My parents hosted the rowdy Christmas Eve "chili party." Making chili was one of mom's early lessons for keeping things simple. She'd put a pot on before church so we could come home for a quick meal, get us kids to bed, and begin a long night of wrapping gifts. In its heyday, the party grew to over forty people. Mom would bedeck the house with decorations, including so many candles that we made a game of who could find and light them all. She'd have a beautiful cheese plate ready to go by the time the others would arrive with their assigned dish, from mac 'n' cheese to dessert. My contribution is a recipe I made the very first time I hosted a holiday party with my bestie, Andi, in Atlanta. Now known as "Holiday Brie," it's topped with brown-sugar-glazed almonds and never disappoints (see page 132).

On Christmas night, we'd do it all over again over at the Tuthills', albeit with a smaller crowd and a more formal meal. Through the years, the next generation inevitably became close friends, and in my case, married and eventually divorced. Lucky for us, we never had the "how to split the holidays" struggle, since we already spent them together. Besides, messing with a Church Lady tradition is simply not an option, so to this day, we make it work, not just for our children but for all of us.

The chili party my mom loved so much has waned in numbers as of late, but you can still count on some of us getting together for Holiday Brie, a bowl of chili, and, of course, a cheese and charcuterie board, which I love doing in the shape of a holiday wreath to make it extra special.

On the Board

CHEESES: Manchego, Brie, mozzarella balls

CHARCUTERIE: Genoa salami, spicy and mild hard salami

EXTRAS: Red and green Cerignola olives, red pearl peppers, almonds, dried and whole oranges, fresh herbs (rosemary, bay leaves, sage)

Create the base of the wreath by placing hardy stems of herbs around the perimeter of a large round platter. I prefer rosemary this time of year because it smells of the season and perfectly mimics pine. Place three small bowls around the circle, spaced evenly. I used snowflake-shaped candy dishes but any ramekin will do. Fill those with small items like olives or nuts. Next, just like you would with ornaments, start decorating the wreath with groupings of various meats and cheeses (see page 44 for how to make salami roses). I chose red, white, and green ingredients and spaced the colors evenly throughout the wreath. Next, add pops of orange with dried and fresh citrus. Fill out the wreath by tucking in more herbs or edible flowers. Serve crackers and bread on the side.

Food Styling Tip

MANCHEGO THREE WAYS

Among my favorite cheeses to eat, Manchego is also a cheese I love to style. With a beautiful rind—a nod to when the cheese was packed with grass before aging—and a perfectly sliceable texture, it can be arranged in any number of ways to create visual interest on a board. As shown here, you can crisscross slices in a row or fan them out. A tad more complicated, remove the rind from the cheese, being careful to leave ¼ inch and the corner intact to create a "frame," then slice the wedge into triangles and return them to the rind in an alternating pattern.

Drink Pairing

HOLIDAY GRASSHOPPER

My in-laws introduced me to the Holiday Grasshopper after a decadent Christmas dinner. Both a milkshake and a cocktail, I didn't think I'd left room but discovered that the combination of ice cream and mint was the perfect ending to an indulgent holiday. Using a blender, mix ¾ cup each of crème de cacao and crème de menthe and 8 scoops ice vanilla or chocolate chip cream for four refreshingly festive cocktails. **Make it a mocktail:** Leave out the crème de cacao and crème de menthe and add just enough milk to thin it out. **Garnish:** Mint makes a sensible garnish for this drink, but if you want to use something on hand, a piece of rosemary adds a holiday touch. To make it even more decadent, add a chocolate-covered pretzel rod, too.

Décor Inspo
CITRUS CENTERPIECE

Around the holidays, it's easy to overlook a few details as you are shuffling between lists of groceries, gifts, and guests. If it's the centerpiece or tabletop décor that fell through the cracks, there are likely more than enough extra supplies lying around to throw together something fabulous. Here, I've tossed some oranges and pears I had on hand into a rustic wooden bowl, clipped branches from the bottom of my Christmas tree, then added a few herbs and branches to fill it out. A glass bowl or tall vase filled with citrus fruit would look equally gorgeous on a side table or on your bar.

Fondue Fete

NEW YEAR'S EVE PROVIDES THE PERFECT EXCUSE to get dressed up, sip champagne, and indulge in rich and fanciful food . . . all from the comfort of your own home, if you're like me. Sure, I danced and partied my way into many a new year back in the day, but after having kids myself, I understand why my parents' ideal New Year's Eve was to stay in with friends and neighbors.

As girls my sister, Martha, and I would sneak downstairs to make a plate of cocktail meatballs and mini quiches, pausing at the bottom of the stairs to eavesdrop. Most of what I remember is their laughter as they sat around the coffee table drinking André, listening to Frankie Valli on the record player, and dunking skewers of bread into a pot of cheese fondue. The tradition they started in the '70s remains, and it's hard for me to imagine serving anything but fondue on New Year's Eve.

Back then, we started requesting fondue for no special occasion at all. Mom would oblige, setting out a platter in the TV room full of cut-up hot dogs and apples and chunks of chewy Italian bread we'd dip into the creamy orange concoction, eyes glued to *M*A*S*H*. I'm not sure exactly when Martha and I realized that the "fondue" we were being served on random weeknights was nothing more than a can of condensed cheddar cheese soup.

I hate to admit it, but as a kid, I liked that version better than the real deal. But that would all change when I moved to Switzerland. There is an art to making traditional fondue there using a mixture of the best Swiss cheeses, garlic, and kirsch, a potent cherry digestif not readily available in the United States, so I often substitute white wine or brandy.

The dish is surprisingly uncomplicated, but there's still no shame in using the vacuum-sealed pouches of premade Swiss fondue available at your supermarket's cheese counter. Just heat it up and it's about as close to the real deal as I've had! Whether you make it or fake it, serve fondue with traditional dippers like bread and fingerling potatoes, along with some cured meat and plenty of cornichons or pickles and a glass of bubbly to balance the richness.

On the Board

CHEESE: Fondue (see page 133 or opt for prepared fondue found in the cheese section of your grocery store)

CHARCUTERIE: Prosciutto

EXTRAS: Boiled fingerling potatoes, French bread, apples, cornichons/pickles

Place a fondue pot or heat-safe crock or ramekin on a large tray or board. If you have one, a lazy Susan is perfect for sharing around a larger table. Add bowls of the various dippers or pile them directly on the tray—I'm all for less dishes to wash! Heat the cheese on the stove directly in the fondue pot or in a saucepan and then transfer to the crock. If you're not using a fondue pot with a heat source, you may have to reheat occasionally on the stove or in the microwave. Serve with picks or skewers. On a separate plate or small platter, arrange a few additional snacks like salty meats, nuts, and pickles.

Food Styling Tip
PROSCIUTTO RIBBONS

One of the questions I get often is how to serve prosciutto. It is best enjoyed sliced thin, making it melt-in-your mouth delicious but also tricky to separate without tearing or ending up with an unappetizing blob. Despite being chided from behind the meat counter, I ask for slightly thicker slices or opt for prepackaged prosciutto divided with small sheets of wax paper. This makes it easy to peel a single slice, as does refrigerating until you're ready to handle it. To create a ribbon effect, fold a single slice of chilled prosciutto longways, then gently fold it back and forth like an accordion. Pinch the bottom while fanning out the folds before placing the slices in a row.

Drink Pairing

GINGER AND PEAR SPARKLER

Bright and refreshing, this sparkling ginger and pear cocktail is an elegant choice for New Year's Eve. You can mix up a batch and serve it in a punch bowl, or for a single cocktail, mix 1 ounce pear nectar with ½ ounce ginger liqueur and top it off with 4 ounces of your favorite champagne or prosecco.

Make it a mocktail: For a bubbly alcohol-free option, replace the liqueur with 2 ounces ginger beer and the champagne with a sparkling white grape juice.

Garnish: Using a toothpick or a sturdy sprig of rosemary, thread a slice of pear and a blackberry for a splash of color in the cocktail.

Décor Inspo

NOISEMAKERS AND PUSHPINS

Before midnight, put those New Year's Eve noisemakers to good use,
gathering them in a glass or vase for an economical decoration. And since
New Year's Eve is all about the bling, turn any plain candles into gold using a
handful of humble pushpins. Here I've embellished orb candles with a pattern
of black and gold ones to match the party's color scheme.

Valentine's Day: Life Is Like a Box of Charcuterie

AT THE RISK OF SOUNDING CYNICAL, I'm not a fan of Valentine's Day in its traditional sense. To me, it means predictable gifts and overcrowded restaurants serving mediocre prix-fixe menus, making it a holiday on which I'd rather opt for a cozy evening in. And, because you know I love a theme, my favorite part of February 14 was the joy my girls found in dousing their heart-shaped pancakes with red sprinkles that morning. Some years we got especially creative and used cookie cutters to make cookies, pizzas, and a heart caprese salad.

In recent years, I've noticed the rise of a related holiday called Galentine's Day, held on February 13. Greeting cards and decorations are popping up

I like you, but I love CHEESE

in stores, apparently making it the official day to celebrate the joy of female friendship. Though I find it equally as cheesy (pun intended) as Valentine's, I love that it originated in *Parks and Recreation* when Leslie says, "Every February 13, my lady friends and I leave our husbands and our boyfriends at home, and we just come and kick it, breakfast-style. Ladies celebrating ladies. It's like Lilith Fair, minus the angst. Plus, frittatas"—and thus a holiday was born. In fact, it has fast become one of the shop's busiest days, including groups of coworkers, family, and friends clamoring for a spot at one of EZPZ's Galentine's Boarding School workshops. If there's one thing I love more than making these adorable charcuterie boxes, it's teaching others how to.

On the Board

CHEESES: Brie with strawberry jam, Manchego, port-wine-soaked Derby, Babybel

CHARCUTERIE: Spicy salami, mild hard salami

EXTRAS: Red Cerignola olives, strawberries, heart cookies

Start with a box of Valentine's Day chocolates in any size you wish. Make a bigger one for a crowd or choose a mini box to create a unique little gift for family, friends, or teachers. Remove the candy (save that for later, of course) and the plastic insert, and line the box with wax paper. Starting with the Brie, use a sharp knife or wire cutter to slice a thin layer of rind off the top (see page 56 for a similar method). Cut out a heart from this layer using a cookie cutter. Before putting it back on top, spread a very thin layer of strawberry jam onto the Brie. Another trick is to use a small cookie cutter to cut hearts in the wax on a small wheel of Gouda or a Babybel cheese. Slice the remaining cheeses and place them, along with hard salami, strawberries, olives, and sweets, in the box before tucking in the show stopper—the infamous salami rose.

Food Styling Tip
THE INFAMOUS SALAMI ROSE

Some people in the charcuterie biz claim the salami rose trend, made popular by TikTok, is dead. But I am here to say it is indeed alive and blooming! As a matter of fact, one time I decided to skip teaching the trick at a workshop, much to my students' disappointment. They begged and I obliged, vowing not to skip the technique again. The key to a perfect rose is choosing a champagne flute or glass that's narrow at the opening. The type of meat you choose is important, too—rather than hard salami, pick a thinly sliced softer one that is pliable but not flimsy. Another tip: Let the salami come to room temperature so that each piece stays folded. Begin by placing the salami over the rim of the glass, half inside and half out. Continue by layering pieces around the rim, pinching them to the form of the glass, until there's no room left in the center. Depending on the size of the glass, eight to ten slices of salami should do. Turn the glass over in your palm and gently lift the glass off the meat to reveal the most perfect salami rose.

Drink Pairing

A COSMO WITH HEART

It's safe to say this sweet and tart concoction is not just a pop culture throwback to the '80s, but rather an established part of the cocktail lexicon. The frothy drink's blush-pink hue makes it perfect for the season. Mix 1½ ounces citron vodka with ¾ ounce each of fresh lime juice, Cointreau, and cranberry juice cocktail. Shake with ice and strain into a glass. **Make it a mocktail:** Mix 1 ounce orange juice, ¾ ounce lime juice, and ½ ounce cranberry juice (not cocktail, unless you like it very sweet). Serve over ice. **Garnish:** These drinks look especially lovely adorned with a strawberry garnish made by slicing strawberries in half and using a mini cookie cutter to create hearts. Place them on a decorative pick, and for a special ombré effect, use specialty pink and white strawberries when in season.

Décor Inspo

GIVE STORE-BOUGHT ROSES SOME LOVE

It may not be the most inspired Valentine's Day gift, but a dozen grocery-store roses can make an extraordinary arrangement with just a little bit of creativity. Start by placing a small vase inside a larger one, leaving a gap that can be filled with any number of seasonal goodies. For Valentine's Day, I chose a bag of heart candies to tuck between the vases. Fill the inner vase with water and give the roses a fresh cut before arranging them along with some added blooms to give it some texture and interest.

Everyday Gathering Boards for Winter

WINTER GETS BUSY, especially with all those holidays that require planning, shopping, and traveling. So on those rare days when you're not hustling and bustling, it's important to enjoy the downtime. A cozy night in can be the perfect excuse to enjoy a Gathering Board without all the fanfare. Unlike those meant for entertaining, these board ideas are meant to inspire simple ways to add fun and flavor to your winter repertoire.

Hot Chocolate Board

In middle school, both my girls were big into "Secret Santa" parties with their friends. They'd each draw a name out of a hat and surprise that person with a small gift. More than once, I hosted their sweet gift exchange—I loved seeing what they'd chosen for each other. They'd arrive in their themed outfits like "ugly sweaters" or holiday PJs and I'd order pizza. For dessert, a cozy hot chocolate board was a fun and interactive treat for the girls. Simply heat up chocolate milk (or make your own hot chocolate) in a crock pot or a saucepan on the stove. Load up a festive platter with plenty of sweet fixings for drizzling, topping, and stirring.

On the Board

HOT CHOCOLATE

TOPPINGS: Candy canes (leave some whole for stirring, crush some for topping), caramel syrup (and/or other coffee syrups like hazelnut, vanilla, or peppermint), chocolate-covered pretzel rods, chocolate-mint candies (crumbled), chocolate syrup, cinnamon sticks, marshmallows (large and/or mini, plain and/or flavored), mini chocolate chips, sprinkles, whipped cream

Baked Potato Board

In my twenties, I lived on baked potatoes. Inexpensive and ready in eight minutes in the microwave, they were one of the meals I "cooked" on a regular basis. I'd top them with cheddar cheese if I had it, or just plain butter and salt. Later in life, my friend Andi and I discovered a pub in Atlanta that served piping hot baked (not microwaved) potatoes along with one of those classic silver condiment carousels filled with sour cream, bacon, and chives. That became our favorite pub snack, and now anytime a restaurant has one of those carrousels, I think of her. That's the inspiration behind this board—gathering basic and imaginative toppings on a platter along with a tray of steaming hot baked potatoes.

On the Board

POTATOES: Baked and sliced in half

VEGGIES: Broccoli, steamed; corn; grape tomatoes, halved; green onions, chopped; peas

CHEESE: Shredded cheese of choice (cheddar, pepper jack, smoked gouda)

PROTEINS:Bacon, cooked and crumbled; ham, diced

CONDIMENTS: Cheese sauce, hot sauce, ranch dressing, sour cream

Movie Night Board

When there's a chill in the air, there's no better way to spend an evening than hunkered down with the family to watch a movie. While picking a flick that everyone agrees on can be tough, deciding on snacks can be easy. If you're like me, you like the classic combo—popcorn and candy. In fact, I love it so much that I've been known to go to the theater not to see a movie, but just for a large bucket of popcorn, no butter for me, and a box of Sno-Caps. This is on my top-five list of snack combos and the inspiration behind this Movie Night Board. If not purchased from a theater, I make a fresh batch of steaming hot popcorn on the stove (I prefer the traditional method over microwave) along with baskets of any favorite store-bought flavored popcorns, like caramel or cheddar. I arrange an assortment of candy and other accompaniments on the coffee table, along with paper bags or bowls, so everyone can make their own favorite combo without missing a scene.

On the Board

POPCORN: Plain and/or flavored

CLASSIC MOVIE THEATER CANDY: Junior Mints, M&M's, Milk Duds, Raisinets, Sno-Caps, Twizzlers

OTHER SNACKS: Fresh fruit (sliced oranges, berries), fruit snacks, pretzel rods and/or soft pretzels

Spring Gathering Boards

FOR ME, SPRING FEVER SETS IN THE FIRST MORNING I take my dog, Millie, for a walk without a jacket. That feeling of lightness and enthusiasm puts an extra pep in my step. I'm sure there are tangible reasons for the energy boost like increased exposure to sunlight and warmer temperatures, but for me it's all about the anticipation of finally getting together with friends after a long winter. For those of us who love to host a party, springtime is idyllic. It provides the perfect combination of beautiful weather and a sense of renewal and rejuvenation, and is the perfect time to get outdoors.

As soon as the temps begin to climb, I'm eager to open the windows, dust off the outdoor furniture, and invite people over for any reason, even just to enjoy a sunlit evening on my front porch with some wine and cheese. I often run off to the garden center prematurely (and I'm no green thumb), anxious to add potted plants and greenery throughout my outdoor entertaining spaces and create an atmosphere that's as breezy as my mood.

Beyond the weather, spring also offers a wealth of seasonal ingredients that are both delicious and healthy. Fresh fruits and vegetables are readily available and can be used to create a variety of appetizers as well as refreshing cocktails that are as beautiful as they are delicious.

Luck of the Irish

AS FAR AS THE MONTHS OF SPRING GO, March gets a bad rap, especially where I'm from in Western Pennsylvania. One day it's sunny and warm enough to put the snow shovel back in the basement, only to wake the next day to find six inches of snow on the ground. Between the resulting mud and infamous potholes, I get why March is considered by many to be the dreariest month of the year. But in my family, it begins with three birthdays—my daughter Lydia on March 2 and my sister and I both on March 5 (I was born on her fourth birthday!).

Then a couple of weeks later, St. Patrick's Day provides the perfect excuse for those itching for a reason to celebrate. Like many holidays, St. Patrick's Day festivities can differ drastically depending on your stage in life. As a kid,

it's all about shamrock cookies, crafts, and anticipating what shenanigans the leprechaun might pull in your classroom. Fast-forward and the day is all about green beer and, in my case, heading to the St. Patrick's Day parade in downtown Pittsburgh. With about 15 percent of the area's population claiming Irish heritage, it is no wonder my hometown boasts one of the largest St. Patrick's Day celebrations in the country. Many memories, as foggy as they may be, were made alongside hundreds of thousands of revelers dressed head to toe in green. It was a daylong affair that began at the top o' the mornin' and ended late in the evening at one of many pubs and bars around town.

Much older and a little wiser, I skip the parade but still celebrate the holiday with a few nods to my Irish heritage, however slight it may be. I take advantage of restaurants offering seasonal specials and bring home a meal like shepherd's pie or Irish stew, and then put together a St. Patty's Gathering Board featuring classic Irish cheeses, of course, along with green and orange goodies for all the lads and lasses.

On the Board

CHEESES: Pesto Gouda, Guinness cheddar, aged Irish cheddar, sage Derby

CHARCUTERIE: Capocollo

EXTRAS: Green Cerignola olives, dried apricots, green grapes, fresh herbs

Start with an orange or green platter, if you have one, and begin arranging your cheeses. To give them some interest, try some sliced in rectangles and triangles and some cubed. Use a cookie cutter and a thin slice of cheese (green if you have it) to make a shamrock, or if you don't have one that shape, use four heart cutouts as leaves to create a four-leaf clover. Roll or lay the charcuterie meats and tuck in green grapes, olives, and dried apricots to fill the board with the quintessential colors of the day.

Food Styling Tip

WAX ON, WAX OFF

Some of the most popular cheeses have waxed rinds. Cheeses like Gouda, for example, are pressed then dipped and sealed in wax before aging. Though any color of wax can coat any type of cheese, the most common shade is red. But for a themed board, it's worth finding a rind that matches—like the green-waxed Irish cheddar. Using a sharp knife or wire cutter, slice along the perimeter of the wedge, following the shape of the rind but leaving a quarter inch of cheese attached to it. Cut the wedge into cubes and pile them back inside the rind "frame."

Drink Pairing

IRISH MULE

There's no shortage of beverages to choose from on St. Patrick's Day, from Guinness to Irish coffee. For something different, try an Irish take on a Moscow Mule made by replacing vodka with Irish whiskey. Combine 2 ounces whiskey, 4 ounces ginger beer, and a few squeezes of fresh lime juice and pour over ice in a copper mug (or any glass). **Make it a mocktail:** In recent years, whiskey mocktails have gone mainstream. There are several high-end brands of whiskey alternatives. Try one of them, or swap in ginger ale for sweetness, and you have a refreshing nonalcoholic drink. **Garnish:** A simple slice of lime and a sprig of mint look pretty and give a hint to this cocktail's contents. Sláinte!

Décor Inspo
PENNY PINCHING

Here's a St. Patty's Day decorating idea that comes together for pennies, literally. I'm always scrounging around last minute for a way to pump up a theme without buying a thing. This time I was looking around the house for copper knickknacks to go with the mule cups when I realized the bottom of my purse held, well, a pot of gold. I dumped out the pennies and started playing with ideas, finding they tucked perfectly inside votive candle holders. Scatter more pennies and gold candy coins for the kiddos on a basket of floral moss for a whimsical tablescape reminiscent of the Irish countryside.

Eat Your Veggies

HERE'S A CONFESSION: Sometimes I tire of meat and cheese, whether it's eating or styling it. Which is why I get excited when a customer asks to accommodate vegetarian or vegan guests, or just wants something on the lighter side. It gives me a chance to work with a different "medium" and create beautiful boards highlighting fresh vegetables.

Springtime is the ideal season for a bountiful vegetable board, what with peas, broccoli, cabbage, carrots, and radishes among the first to be harvested. Asparagus is another spring veggie and one of my favorites. I was thrilled to discover in Switzerland that restaurants officially celebrate *Spargelzeit* (asparagus season) in early spring, with entire menus devoted to it. One of the most memorable dishes was a classic Swiss preparation of white asparagus, sweetened with a bit of sugar and served with new potatoes and butter (see page 134).

But let's get back to veggie boards or crudités, a French word that loosely translates to "raw things," often dipped in a light dip or sauce. Store-bought or homemade, dressings and hummus are a great choice. In my house, it's always Mom's "famous" dill dip (see page 135). If there's not already a container of it in my fridge, I keep the ingredients handy so I can whip some up for a midday snack with vegetables, pretzels, or crackers. It also makes a refreshing and creamy accompaniment for hot or cold salmon.

Styling vegetables is a lot like putting flowers in a vase—if you choose a variety of fresh and colorful ones, they'll look gorgeous with little effort. To dress it up a bit, line the platter with some colorful lettuce leaves or kale. Place the dips first, then start layering vegetables around them. You can make groupings by type or by color, putting all the red, orange, and green veggies together. Here I've opted to distribute the colors and textures throughout for a more organic look. Sprigs of fresh herbs and edible flowers give the arrangement a fresh-from-the-garden feel.

On the Board

DIPS: Mom's dill dip, store-bought hummus

VEGETABLES: Purple kale, bell peppers, rainbow carrots, baby zucchini, grape tomatoes, cucumbers, snap peas, celery, rainbow cauliflower, radishes

Begin by washing, slicing, and preparing all of the ingredients. For a nice variety, slice some veggies longways, like the carrots and zucchini, and others into rounds. Line a platter with leaves of kale or lettuce. A flat tray will do, but a deeper platter or bowl gives it a more bountiful look. Build the arrangement starting with the dips at the center. I added the celery core, because it looked too lovely to toss out, and surrounded it with the cauliflower. Then, working from the outside in, begin layering your long-cut veggies. You can choose to group them by type, mix them all up, or do a bit of both. Once you get close to the center, fill in empty spaces with piles of tomato and cucumber florets. Tuck in any round slices of cucumbers and radishes and finish with snap peas, sprigs of fresh herbs, and edible flowers.

Food Styling Tip
CUCUMBER FLORETS

This is a tried-and-true trick I use to level up any veggie board or salad. All you need is a mandolin (or a sharp knife and a steady hand) and at least two seedless cucumbers. Start by making the cups by cutting as many ½-inch-thick slices as you are making florets. Carve the flesh out of each slice to create the cups. Next, thinly slice another cucumber and layer several circles in a row. Roll the thin slices to form the flower and tuck it into one of the cups, then gently separate the "petals." You can try this trick with thin slices of lemons, limes, and oranges, too.

Drink Pairing
CUCUMBER BASIL MARTINI

Muddle three or four slices of cucumber and basil leaves in a cocktail shaker. Add 2 teaspoons simple syrup, 1 ounce St. Germain liqueur, 2 ounces of your favorite gin, and a squeeze of lemon or lime juice (or both). Add crushed ice and give it a good shake. Strain into a glass with or without ice. **Make it a mocktail:** Try this lemony twist by muddling cucumber and basil in a glass, adding ice, and topping off with lemonade and a bit of club soda. **Garnish:** Using a mandolin or sharp knife, cut a very thin slice of cucumber lengthwise. Roll it into a rosette or fan it back and forth to create a ribbon effect and skewer onto a pick. Add an edible flower and/or a mint leaf for color.

Décor Inspo

VEGGIE VASE

I get a kick out of using food in unexpected ways. I came up with this asparagus vase for a Christmas party, but I love it even more during asparagus season. To create, trim asparagus to be the same height as a cylindrical vase. Place a thick rubber band around the vase, using one that's just loose enough to leave space for the asparagus. Tuck the spears in one by one until the vase is fully covered. To hide the rubber band, tie a ribbon around the asparagus, then add water and drop in your favorite spring blooms.

Mother's Day Brunch Basket

FOR A STRETCH IN THE 1990s, long before I was a mom myself, Mother's Day was spent walking with the Church Ladies—the nickname for my mom and her dearest friends—and their daughters in the annual Susan G. Komen Race for the Cure, which raised funds and awareness about breast cancer. We'd meet early and bleary-eyed in our matching "Church Lady" T-shirts along with over 20,000 runners and walkers. The race ambled the streets of Pittsburgh, giving us lots of time to catch up, laugh, and get in a little exercise before heading for brunch and mimosas, of course.

Ravenous from our walk (it was slow, but the hills!), we'd eat and drink . . . and drink well into the afternoon, our race bibs still attached to our bright orange Church Lady shirts with "It's a long story" emblazoned on the back. Indeed, the story of this multigenerational gaggle of women was a long one. And little did we know then that breast cancer would become part of our story, along with other ailments, some terminal.

The last time I walked in the Race for the Cure was in 2004, the first time as a new mom . . . and the last time with *my* mom. The following year, she was way too sick to walk but insisted on brunch. We were all together, drinking mimosas and laughing as usual. That was the last time I saw her alive.

Mother's Day took on a deeper and more emotional meaning after that. But the need to be together with the women that meant so much to her was stronger than ever. And now that the next generation of Church Ladies was having babies, a casual brunch on my back deck became a better alternative to the race and boisterous afternoon out.

A basket piled high with sweet and savory goodies is a thoughtful and stress-free brunch. Naturally, I don't bake but rather purchase pastries, muffins, and mini bagels and serve them with a choice of spreads, smoked salmon, and other toppings. Round out the basket with fresh fruit, and you've got plenty of choices to please all the moms in your life.

On the Board

BAKED GOODS: Bagels, biscotti, croissants, muffins, scones

PROTEIN: Smoked salmon

SPREADS: Creamed cheese, goat cheese

TOPPINGS: Capers, tomatoes

Line a basket or platter with a colorful cloth or paper napkin. Place the salmon and goat cheese on small plates, and spoon cream cheese and smaller berries into mason jars or ramekins. Place those items in the basket and begin adding the baked goods—I chose mini bagels and bite-size muffins because they are easy to eat and allow for more variety. Fill in with fresh fruit, herbs, and edible flowers.

Food Styling Tip
GARDEN GOAT CHEESE LOGS

This is a remarkably easy and stunning presentation using edible flowers (like lavender, pansies, or marigolds) and herbs, either fresh from your garden or store-bought. With a plain or herbed goat cheese log (see page 136) as your canvas, create a unique work of art using flower petals and chopped or whole herbs. Spread on bagels, crackers, or sliced baguette.

Drink Pairing

LAVENDER MOMOSA

A little sweet with a hint of floral notes, this beautiful bubbly cocktail pairs with a light brunch. Pour ¼ ounce fresh lemon juice and ½ ounce lavender syrup (Torani makes one, or create your own by infusing simple sugar with dried lavender) into a champagne glass and top with your favorite champagne or prosecco. **Make it a mocktail:** This drink is just as festive using the same ingredients but replacing the champagne with club soda or, for a sweeter drink, sparkling white grape juice. **Garnish:** A fresh sprig of lavender makes a simple garnish. For a distinctive presentation, use a miniature clothespin found at the craft store to affix the lavender to the glass.

Décor Inspo

PICTURE-PERFECT PLANTS

Around Mother's Day, beautifully wrapped potted plants are easy to come by at garden centers and grocery stores. They make a thoughtful gift as is, but with a personal touch, like a photo of mom, they double as centerpiece and gift. Ask the floral department for a couple plastic card holders to tuck photographs, kid's artwork, or a poem or message.

Everyday Gathering Boards for Spring

SPRINGTIME OFFERS SO MANY REASONS TO CELEBRATE, my favorite of which is no reason at all. The rising temperatures and lengthening daylight are all the excuse I need to spend time on the porch enjoying fresh air and good food. Using the same concepts and methods previously described, you can create everyday Gathering Boards for impromptu spring get-togethers, easy dinners, or just a delicious snack.

Mediterranean Board

In Pittsburgh, the month of May marks the beginning of Greek Food Festival season, when Greek Orthodox churches throughout the region celebrate with dancing, live music, vendors, and, of course, amazing food. Having traveled in Greece, these festivals transport me right back to a sun-soaked beach on Crete or a bustling cliffside taverna on Santorini. It was during that trip that I discovered, among other delicacies, tzatziki—a cucumber yogurt dip that is as popular in Greece as ketchup is in the United States. Back then, the dip was not yet popular here, so I perfected a recipe (see page 138) to serve with warm pita when I need a fix. Today, tzatziki and the region's other popular dishes can be found in most supermarkets, making a Mediterranean Board one of my favorite appetizers or, with grilled chicken or lamb, a light meal. I start by placing bowls of dips, nuts, olives, and feta on the board and then arrange the fruits and vegetables. Next I place the stuffed grape leaves (I prefer them at room temp), baked spanakopita, and warmed pita bread and invite friends to dig in.

On the Board

DOLMAS: Stuffed grape leaves, often found in cans near olives

CHEESE: Feta (block or crumbled)

DIPS: Hummus, tzatziki

BAKED GOODS: Pita bread, sliced into triangles; spanakopita (phyllo layers filled with spinach and feta cheese, often found in the frozen section)

VEGGIES: Greek olives; cherry tomatoes, halved; cucumbers, sliced

FRUITS AND NUTS: Fresh figs or fig preserves, grapes, pistachios

Salad Bar Board

Ask any of my high school friends about my go-to order at Wendy's and they'd remember, "Garden Spot, medium Diet Coke." I've always loved a salad bar, even if it was bare bones at a fast-food place. Then when my college roommate Laura and I went to Boulder, Colorado, for the summer, we discovered a restaurant called Healthy Habits and I thought I'd died and gone to salad bar heaven. Picture what seemed like a mile-long meandering display featuring every ingredient you might imagine goes on or with a salad. I often say that if I could, I'd replace my dining room table with a fully functioning salad bar. But instead, when the mood strikes, I create a mini version with a big bowl of fresh greens and any toppings I have on hand, from sweet and salty to creamy and crunchy. Whether it's a quick dinner aimed at getting rid of leftovers or an elegant and effortless luncheon, this Salad Bar Board never fails to impress. Here is just a sample of the many ingredients you can include.

On the Board

VEGETABLES: Asparagus, broccoli, carrots, cauliflower, cherry tomatoes, corn, cucumbers, leafy greens (romaine, spinach, mixed greens), mushrooms, onions, peas, radishes

PICKLED/MARINATED: Artichokes, beets, mushrooms

FRUITS: Apples; berries (blueberries, strawberries, blackberries); mandarin oranges; peaches, plums, and/or pears, sliced; raisins and/or dried cranberries

CHEESES (CRUMBLED, SHAVED, OR SLICED): Blue, feta, mozzarella, Parmesan

PROTEINS: Black beans, chicken, garbanzo beans, hard-boiled eggs, salmon, shrimp, steak, tofu, tuna

CRUNCH: Almonds, sliced; crispy noodles; croutons; pepitas; sesame sticks; sunflower seeds; walnuts, chopped

DRESSINGS: Lemon slices, olive oil and vinegar (red wine, balsamic), premade Italian, blue cheese, ranch, poppy seed, etc.

Biscuit Board

When my elder daughter graduated high school, we threw a party and served southern food in honor of her decision to attend the College of Charleston in South Carolina. The low country boasts plenty of specialties, a favorite of which is flaky, buttery biscuits. So for her party, we created a "Biscuit Bar" where guests could add all kinds of toppings. Re-creating a smaller but equally delectable biscuit board at home is simple, whether you make them yourself or purchase biscuits from your favorite bakery or market. The board can be taken in a sweet or savory direction (or both), with ingredients ranging from sausage and cheese to fruit and honey.

On the Board

BISCUITS

SAVORY: Bacon; baked ham and/or turkey, carved; sausage patties; cheddar cheese, shredded or sliced; cranberry relish or sauce; herbed butter; hot sauce; mustard (honey and/or whole grain)

SWEET: Apple butter, butter, fruit jams or preserves, honey, nutella, peanut butter, seasonal fresh fruit

Summer Gathering Boards

SUMMER IS THE QUINTESSENTIAL SEASON for outdoor entertaining. From Memorial Day to Labor Day and everything in between—including my daughter Edie's birthday—in summer there is no shortage of reasons to throw a party.

When it comes to food, this season is all about fresh ingredients. Even a dinner party comes together easily with some grilled meat, refreshing salads, and plenty of cold drinks. When it's just too hot to cook, I opt for a board filled with a bounty of cheese, meat, fruits, and nuts that, in summer, stands in for a meal with little complaint!

Simple and summery decorations like colorful tablecloths and napkins, lanterns, and some fresh blooms are all you need to create an easy, breezy atmosphere. Summer entertaining is all about enjoying the company of friends and family in a relaxed and beautiful setting. Whether it's a backyard barbecue or an elegant dinner, there are plenty of simple ways to make summer gatherings a success.

Red, White, and "Bleu"

I FEEL INCREDIBLY LUCKY to still live and work in Aspinwall, the quaint sidewalk community just east of Pittsburgh. My dad is still in the house in which he and my mom raised us, and my sister and I have since raised our kids here, just two blocks from each other. It's the kind of place where we keep an eye out for everyone's children, shovel each other's sidewalks, and a short walk can take an hour because you inevitably stop to chat with neighbors.

Established in 1892, Aspinwall is dubbed "The Town That Pride Built" and that pride is never more evident than on Memorial Day. Each year, our annual neighborhood parade snakes through the tree-lined streets to the delight of kids and adults alike. Patriotic bunting and American flags abound to honor our heroes and signal that summer is near. Lawn chairs start to appear along the parade route as early as 9:00 a.m., which around here is not too early for the backyard or porch parties to get underway.

The parade showcases army reservists, borough police and volunteer firefighters, Boy and Girl Scouts, cheerleaders, and marching bands. Each group tosses candy to the eager little ones dressed in their best patriotic outfits, who are invited to follow behind the parade on bicycles. When I was a kid, we proudly and painstakingly decorated our bikes from wheels to handlebars in red, white, and blue crepe paper. By the end of the parade, there were hundreds of us peddling along proudly.

The parade is short and sweet, but the celebration continues well into the afternoon as kids wander the streets with their friends and adults stroll from party to party. My house is off the parade route by about a block, so we often venture to friends' porches and bring along a platter of this or a pitcher of that. My favorite way to contribute to the festivities is to arrive with some of these patriotic cups, filled to the brim with all things red, white, and "bleu."

On the Board

CHEESES: Blue, Gouda, mini Brie, port-wine-soaked Derby

CHARCUTERIE: Mini salami, hard salami

EXTRAS: Red pearl peppers, strawberries, blackberries, almonds

Start by filling each cup with almonds or berries to make a steady base in which to tuck the other components. You can use any combo of cheese, meat, fruit, and peppers to make three different skewers. Choose firm cheeses like Gouda or a half of a mini Brie for the picks, and tuck soft or crumbly ones directly into the cup at the end.

Food Styling Tip
MAKE IT A MINI

At the shop, our single-serve options are incredibly popular. We do all sorts including palm leaf cones and boats, as well as "jarcuterie" served in adorable little mason jars. I also love these themed paper cups that you can find at a party supply store. And matching picks like these gold balls are a fun addition, too—you can find them in just about any color or shape ranging from animals and flowers to sports themes. You can also choose foods that match the occasion, like the red, white, and blue ingredients for Memorial Day. No matter what you put them in, mini charcuterie makes a sensible snack for a crowd on warm days since you can use a variety of ingredients and keep them in the fridge to replenish throughout the day as needed.

Drink Pairing

BLUEBERRY MOJITO

This is a refreshing twist on the classic Cuban cocktail in a color befitting the holiday. Muddle a handful of blueberries and a few mint leaves in a glass. Add ice, then pour in 2 ounces white rum, 1 ounce simple syrup, and a squeeze of lime juice. Stir and then top with sparkling water and a garnish of blueberries, mint, and lime. **Make it a mocktail:** Follow the instructions above, but instead of rum try making this drink with sparkling water or kombucha. **Garnish:** Skewer several blueberries to cover a long pick to place in or on top of the glass. Finish with a sprig of fresh mint and a colorful straw.

Décor Inspo

THE COBALT BLUES

At one point in time, I started collecting cobalt blue medicine bottles I'd find in antique shops. I loved the way they looked gathered together on my mantel or windowsill. Then I discovered a spring water that comes in a gorgeous blue glass bottle, so I started stockpiling those, too. I've used the collection for countless centerpieces, and filled with red or white flowers they make a great addition to a patriotic table.

Picnic in the Park

I JUST LOVE A PICNIC! Sometimes I imagine throwing a fanciful "party of pleasure" like the grand picnics Jane Austen portrays in books like *Sense and Sensibility*, my absolute favorite novel and film. I picture platters of meat and fish, bountiful bowls of berries, and dainty pastries all laid out on white blankets under a canopy of trees in the countryside.

I must admit to channeling my inner Ms. Dashwood when I pack a basket and head to Hartwood Acres, a historical sixteenth-century-style Tudor mansion outside of Pittsburgh. With lush acreage of trees and green fields, it would indeed be the perfect setting for a Jane Austen–style fete—that is, if it weren't for the rock bands or the crowd of fans gathered on lawn chairs who, like me, flock there for the free summer concerts.

There's just something about fresh air and a fresh perspective that makes food taste better. This dawned on me when I hosted a late-summer dinner party in my thirties. My dining room was small for the group, but it was one of those rare August evenings with a nice breeze, so we threw a spare rug in the backyard, dragged a table outside, and strung some lights on the branches above. Though we were only a few yards from my dining room, it felt as if we were miles away. We must have stayed out sipping wine and chatting for hours. I can't be sure what I "cooked" that evening, but I have a hunch it was my go-to summer salmon Niçoise salad, made entirely from premade dishes from the prepared counter at my local grocery store (see page 137). If memory serves, it tasted better than ever simply because we were outside under the stars.

I taught my kids the joy of eating al fresco early on, when they thought it was such a treat to go on a "picnic" (aka tossing a towel down at the park to enjoy a juice box and snacks from the vending machine). Of course, it is fun to get a tad fancier than that, which for me means little more than swapping out the towel for a proper blanket and choosing an assortment of wholesome food all wrapped up in a pretty basket like the one I found at a yard sale.

On the Board

CHEESES: Goat cheese log (plain or herbed), sharp cheddar, fresh mozzarella balls (cherry size)

CHARCUTERIE: Genoa salami, prosciutto

EXTRAS: Pitted olives, seasonal berries, baguette or crackers, basil

While a large platter would work, for easier transport consider making and serving this feast right out of lidded glass or plastic containers. You can put each ingredient in its own container or create individual grazing boxes for one or to share. Slice the cheeses into bite-size pieces and line them up along with rows of charcuterie meat and fresh berries. Serve with summer caprese sticks (see below) and a baguette. I don't even bother slicing it— just tear it up and dig in!

Food Styling Tip

SUMMER ON A STICK

Not only do they make for mess-free picnicking, but these cute little skewers take the guesswork out of what goes with what. For a summer spin on a caprese salad, swap out the tomato for a slice of juicy peach, paired with basil, prosciutto, and a mozzarella ball (*ciliegine*, which means "cherry," is the perfect size).

Drink Pairing

MASON JAR SANGRIA

Mason jars make the perfect vessel for individual cocktails-to-go and can be found in just about any supermarket or craft store. Place a few slices of seasonal fruit in each half-pint mason jar. Add 4 ounces white wine (I prefer sauvignon blanc or pinot grigio in summer) and 2 ounces white rum. If you like it sweet, add a teaspoon of sugar or a spoonful of lemonade or orange juice concentrate. Screw on the lids, give the jars a shake, and let the fruit marinate in the refrigerator for a few hours or overnight. Pack them up and when you're ready to enjoy, add ice and top off with chilled soda water. **Make it a mocktail:** Choose a white grape juice instead of wine, and when topped off with soda after the fruit marinates, you've got a perfect picnic refresher. **Garnish:** With all that lovely fruit, a simple slice of citrus and a colorful straw are all the garnish this drink requires.

Décor Inspo

PICNIC PROPS

It's fairly simple to level up a basic picnic spread without spending a dime. Start with a color scheme and shop around your house for a blanket and some fun throw pillows for comfort and style. Dig out complementary napkins, plates, and placemats. If you don't have a portable camping table, bring along a large board or tray—any low, flat surface will do. And for a memorable touch, bring an extra mason jar and fill it up with wildflowers, river rocks, shells, or anything else you find along your picnic journey.

Lakeside Snackle Box

IF YOU HAD TO CHOOSE, are you a lake person or a beach person? While so many of my friends crave the sea and sand, I fall squarely in the lake column. I'm way more at home on a dock than a beach towel, tolerate rocks over sand, and prefer to swim without fear of riptides or jellyfish. I am a true lake girl, the product of growing up spending summers at Chautauqua Lake in New York. My grandparents discovered the tranquil vacation spot when my mom and aunt were teens, which makes me a "third-generation Chautauquan."

In June, we'd pack up the station wagon, tie the bikes to the roof, and head there for six weeks, sharing a cottage with my aunt, uncle, and their

three boys. It was the kind of place we'd go to, in today's terms, unplug. No TV to entertain us, just a cassette recorder, a deck of cards, and the endless adventures provided by seventeen miles of lakeshore. The kind of place where we'd disappear on our bikes with our cousins, only returning to the house for a fluffernutter sandwich before heading to University Beach for a swim.

Chautauqua was and remains idyllic, and we are lucky to be raising the fourth generation of lake lovers at the home my parents purchased in 1987. Days are spent reading under the shade, cooled by a breeze, and watching the kids play in the lake as boats sail by. Each evening begins on the deck with a cocktail and some combination of cheese, meat, and nuts. Nothing fancy, but just enough to tide us over while we fire up the grill, shuck the corn, and make a quick tomato-cucumber salad (see page 139).

Full disclosure: Our cocktail hours are not typically this clever. But I love a theme as well as an unconventional way to serve food, so when I found a tackle box, rarely used since the kids stopped fishing, I had an idea. Why not fill it (after a thorough cleaning, of course) with snacks and call it a "snackle" box! It makes for a perfect Father's Day or birthday party treat, or an ingenious way to transport snacks for a boat outing or picnic on the dock.

On the Board

CHEESES: Smoked Gouda, balsamic cheddar, Guinness cheddar

CHARCUTERIE: Hard salami, peppered salami

EXTRAS: Green olives, red pearl peppers, berries, grapes, almonds, crackers, pretzels

If you can't find a traditional tackle box, a great alternative is a plastic craft box with compartments that can be found at a craft store. Here, I've used the small compartments on the top tier for smaller items like hard salami, cheeses, and pretzels. The larger lower compartment is great for a big bunch of grapes, some crackers, and jars of berries and nuts. Arrange the ingredients in a way that leaves room for you to close the box for transport, then rearrange if needed once open.

Food Styling Tip
RUSTIC CRUMBLES

While some cheeses are more sliceable, others just fall apart if you don't let them come down to room temperature before cutting. When that happened, I used to toss the chards into my "lunch bowl" for nibbling on later. Then during a class, a student having the same problem said, "I'm going to put these in a pile and call them rustic." We all laughed, but it stuck. Behold the beauty of rustic crumbles! These are particularly helpful with aged cheeses like Parmesan that naturally have less moisture and those that are hard to slice, like balsamic cheddar and Guinness-soaked cheddar.

Drink Pairing

BOURBON ARNOLD PALMER

My dad isn't big into fishing, but he sure does love golf, so I whipped up a classic cocktail named after one of the sport's greatest, Arnold Palmer. Made by mixing half lemonade and half iced tea, add a shot of your favorite bourbon and a sprig of mint for a light summer cocktail. For the tea, this time of year, I load a pitcher of water with bags of plain black tea, leaving it on the deck to steep slowly in the sun. Somehow sun tea just tastes better. **Make it a mocktail:** The Arnold Palmer originated as a nonalcoholic drink named for the American golfer who was known to request the beverage combination. Leave out the bourbon for a delightful summer drink, one of my kids' favorites. **Garnish:** For a twist on a lemon garnish, cut a lemon into thin slices and then make a slit in each slice, cutting from the middle to the edge of the slice. Twist one side of the lemon forward and the other backward, then thread onto a toothpick.

Décor Inspo
DIY BURLAP BANNER

When you're celebrating an occasion, one way to give the guest of honor a shout-out is with a rudimentary sign or banner. Nothing fancy, this one is made of burlap cutouts and twine, which fits with the rustic lake theme. Rummage around in the craft bin for fabric or simply use paper cut into triangles or flag shapes to create a personalized message for your special guest.

Everyday Gathering Boards for Summer

THERE ARE PLENTY OF REASONS TO ENTERTAIN during the summer, but you don't need an occasion to put the Gathering Board methods to good use. Quick summer sides, no-cook meals, and nutritious breakfasts are as beautiful as they are easy when you display the ingredients in pretty bowls on a large platter. Use these board ideas to inspire your own ideas for feeding the family on those long, hot summer days.

Yogurt Parfait Board

I remember exactly where I was when I had my first yogurt parfait. It was in the late '80s in San Diego during a weeklong conference for UPS, the company where I worked for several years. Before each day's meetings began, the hotel put out the usual Danish and donuts, but this colorful concoction of yogurt, fresh fruit, and crunchy granola was out of this world. California, after all, was ahead of the food trends, and I've been making them for breakfast ever since. When bowls of yogurt and granola are offered on a board filled with summer's bounty of fruit, it makes for a tasty breakfast for a crowd, a light lunch, or even dessert. It's sweet, salty, creamy, and crunchy . . . not to mention so easy to pull together. I love having guests make their parfaits in mason jars so you can see all the different combos and layers everyone creates.

On the Board

GRANOLA: Choose from any number of flavors at the store

GREEK YOGURT: Plain and/or flavored

FRESH FRUITS: Bananas, sliced; blackberries; blueberries; peaches, sliced; red raspberries; strawberries, sliced

CRUNCH: Chocolate chips or coco nibs, dried cranberries or raisins, pecans and/or sliced almonds

SWEETENERS: Agave syrup, honey

Crostini Board

Meaning "little toasts" in Italian, crostini are slices of rustic bread toasted and brushed with olive oil and garlic. They make a perfect vehicle for sweet and savory toppings, most commonly bruschetta made with diced tomatoes, fresh basil, and a sprinkle of salt and pepper. In addition to classic bruschetta, place additional toppings and spreads on a big board and you've got a gorgeous presentation that bursts with color and flavors. Many of these spreads are simple to whip up from scratch in summer when tomatoes, vegetables, and herbs are at their peak. Or opt for prepared versions of bruschetta, pesto, and olive tapenade found in the store's canned or prepared food aisle. Add your choice of spreadable cheeses, fresh and marinated vegetables, proteins, and glazes and enjoy experimenting with the endless combinations.

On the Board

CROSTINI: Toasted rustic bread slices drizzled with olive oil and rubbed with garlic

SPREADS: Olive tapenade, pesto, tomato bruschetta

CHEESES: Fresh mozzarella, sliced; fresh ricotta and/or cottage cheese; goat cheese (plain and/or flavored)

PROTEINS: Bacon, prosciutto

VEGGIES: Avocado, sliced; caramelized onions; cucumber, sliced; marinated artichokes, sliced

FRUITS: Fresh figs or fig preserves; peaches, sliced

FINISHING TOUCHES: Balsamic glaze; fresh basil or other herbs, chopped; spicy honey

Corn on the Cob Board

Have I mentioned how much my family loves corn on the cob? Growing up, summer dinners always included at least a dozen ears for the four of us, grown in fields down the street from our home in Chautauqua, New York. With corn that fresh, just a bit of butter or salt does the trick, but sometimes it's fun to kick it up a notch, especially when having friends over for a BBQ. This Corn on the Cob Board makes a simple, summery, and scrumptious side. Use your favorite method for cooking the corn (I prefer boiling) and set the steaming ears on a platter along with a variety of butters, condiments, dried seasonings, and more.

On the Board

CORN ON THE COB

BUTTERS: Herbed butter (mix fresh herbs with softened butter), salted butter (I just put a stick of butter on a plate and let 'em roll)

OTHER SPREADS AND CONDIMENTS: BBQ sauce, hot pepper jelly, pesto, spicy honey

CHEESES (SHREDDED): Cheddar, Parmesan

SEASONINGS: Chili lime, curry powder, fresh chopped herbs (rosemary, basil, cilantro, parsley), Old Bay

Fall Gathering Boards

FOR ME, THE ANSWER TO "WHAT'S YOUR FAVORITE SEASON?" is a toss-up between spring and fall. Both conjure up a sense of change and anticipation. Like spring, I love fall's milder temps, plus the spectacular show Mother Nature puts on as summer's green foliage turns a fiery orange and red. I'm a sucker for a local pumpkin patch or harvest festival, with all the corn mazes, hayrides, and apple cider I can get. Add to that a good old-fashioned bonfire on a crisp fall evening, and I'm a happy camper.

Autumn weather also motivates me to gather friends together. As the leaves change and the weather cools down, I can't help but think of an excuse for one last backyard party or start planning cozy indoor get-togethers featuring autumn's flavors and colors.

No matter what the incentive, be it a football game, Halloween, or Thanksgiving, the bounty of seasonal food and décor makes fall entertaining easy. With little more than an impressive appetizer board, a few mums, and a plaid tablecloth, you have the makings of a festive fall gathering.

Game-Day Tailgate Box

IT WAS VIRTUALLY IMPOSSIBLE NOT TO BE A SPORTS FANATIC growing up in Pittsburgh the '70s. That was, after all, the era when my hometown was dubbed "The City of Champions." I have fond memories memorizing the Pirates' lineup and of dad quizzing us on the colors and mascots of every NFL team. In addition to loving the Pirates, Penguins, and Steelers, my sister and I were groomed young to be die-hard Pitt football fans. We rarely missed a home game, after which we'd walk to a family friend's home where there was table of food that, as a kid, seemed infinite. Sure, donning my blue and gold to go cheer on the Panthers was fun, but the promise of Aunt Jane's postgame deviled eggs and chocolate chip cookies kept my enthusiasm for Pitt football alive and well into my teens.

I suppose that's why when Martha and I both went off to rival Penn State in the 1980s, we never felt like true-blue Nittany Lions fans, not even after winning a national championship. Neither of us had any trouble, however, enjoying the infamous Penn State tailgate parties. Few can deny that we have one of the greatest tailgating traditions of any college team in the country. Decked in blue and white, thousands flock there with coolers filled with food and booze on game days, when Beaver Stadium is said to become the fourth-largest city in Pennsylvania! While some fraternities and alumnae went all out, the student tailgates that I remember consisted of little more than chips and a keg of IC Light, and often continued long after the game was over.

These days, I still use just about any type of sporting event or concert as an excuse to tailgate. But while I do love chips and a cold beer, my spreads take their cues from Aunt Jane's parties rather than my college days. I could never re-create those deviled eggs or cookies, but I hope my cheese and charcuterie box and a batch of Bloodies are equally tempting, even if it's just for watching a game from the comfort of our couch.

In the Box

CHEESES: Smoked Gouda, Manchego, cheddar, balsamic cheddar, ghost pepper Jack

CHARCUTERIE: Spicy and mild salami

EXTRAS: Grapes, cornichons, red pearl peppers, candied nuts

I love bringing this box to a tailgate—no lugging a fragile platter around, plus easy cleanup—but it certainly can be created on a board or plastic tray that represents your team's colors. Start by making the salami football (see below), then slice or cube the cheeses so they're easy to grab. I chose a color palette of brown using the balsamic-soaked and smoked cheeses and added some spice with pepper Jack and spicy salami. Tuck these in around the ball, leaving some out to use for skewers on the Bloody bar. Finish off with grapes, peppers, nuts, and fresh herbs.

Food Styling Tip

MEAT "BALL"

Salami slices topped with provolone "laces" is an abstract but fun trick for game day. Start by folding two round slices of salami in half and then in half again, layering one over the other, pairing them together like a chain link. Line several pairs up in a short row and top with slim slices of provolone to create the laces. Use this folding method without the cheese to make longer rows or a "salami chain" that meanders across your entire board.

Drink Pairing

CLASSIC BLOODY MARY

I whip up a big batch of Bloodies using store-bought mix and vodka and let my guests take it from there. Provide a selection of hot sauces, horseradish, salt, pepper, and dry spice blends to create their perfect drink. **Make it a mocktail**: The so-called Virgin Mary (everything but the vodka) gives you all the spice and tang of a Bloody and is both healthy and filling with all those tasty garnishes. **Garnish:** For me, the Bloody Mary is all about the garnish, which can be a meal in and of itself. I've seen the classic cocktail adorned with everything from shrimp and bacon to an actual mini burger! Anything goes, but keep it practical by creating a DIY garnish bar using some of the same items from the cheese and charcuterie board, along with the perfunctory celery, some pickled veggies, and a selection of hot sauces.

Décor Inspo
GAME-TIME TABLE

Whether it's a coffee table, kitchen island, or an old plastic folding table you dig out from the trunk of your car, give it the proper game-day treatment with items you might already have on hand. Create a runner with craft paper or a black and white cloth and top it with brown bottles made to look like footballs using household masking tape. I used an antique glass vase, but any brown beer bottle with the label removed will do just fine. Throw in some greens, flowers, and/or pennants that represent your team's colors.

CharBOOterie

DID YOU KNOW that next to Super Bowl Sunday, Halloween is the busiest night for pizza delivery? I guess that means not everyone grew up like me eating sloppy joes and tater tots before heading out to trick-or-treat. A tradition I carry on to this day, it makes for a quick and satiating meal, one that parents admit to looking forward to as much as their kiddos.

Even though my children have long outgrown trick-or-treating, Halloween remains one of my favorite celebrations. Rain or shine, adults gather on porches, often with a cocktail and a cozy blanket, as the sidewalks fill with trick-or-treaters. If the weather is good, we can get over three hundred of them! Our first year in the neighborhood, we were unprepared for the onslaught and resorted to handing out granola bars and even oatmeal packets, much to the kids' disappointment, I'm sure.

Centrally located, my house is a popular pit stop on Halloween, so I've learned to be ready for a crowd. Along with the perfunctory sloppy joes and tater tots my friends and family have come to expect, I load up on plenty of wine (parents need treats, too!) and have savory snacks to counter all that sugar. Besides, it gives me an excuse to create a spooky but satisfying appetizer spread.

On the Board

CHEESES: Brie, Port Salut, Cotswold with onions and chives, mild cheddar, ghost pepper Jack, port-wine-soaked Derby

CHARCUTERIE: Hard salami, peppered salami, prosciutto

EXTRAS: Red and green grapes, blackberries, blueberries, dried apricots, pitted green olives, green and purple cauliflower

Choose a variety of meats and cheeses in colors of the holiday—veiny purples and speckled oranges, with pops of green and black. Create a goat cheese grave by spooning red fruit or pepper jam on top and drizzling it with bone candy. Stabbing it with a spreader, preferable a cleaver-shaped one, makes it especially gruesome. Add the Brie mummy (see below) and a hunk of cheddar and Port Salut, orange rind showing. Line up the charcuterie meats and finish off with grapes and the cauliflower I chose exclusively for the color. Top it off with plastic spiders or other decorations, but be sure to let guests know they aren't edible! A few pumpkin-shaped cookies, candy eyes, a gory goat cheese grave, and a Brie mummy make a frighteningly fun feast.

Food Styling Tip
MUMMIFIED BRIE

Remove the top layer of the Brie rind using a wire cutter or sharp knife. Slice the rind into narrow strips and begin laying about half of them back on top of the Brie and trim as needed. Add candy (I found these in the baking aisle) or sliced black olives for eyes.

Drink Pairing

BLACK SANGRIA

This spooky sangria is not only a crowd-pleaser but is easy to whip up for a large group. Combine a bottle of fruity red wine (I like pinot noir) with ¼ cup of brandy, and toss in any fruit you have on hand. Green grapes, blackberries, and citrus slices add a sinister touch. For serving, top with ginger ale. **Make it a mocktail:** Filled with the same fruits and topped with sparkling red grape juice, nonalcoholic sangria is as delicious as it is beautiful. **Garnish:** Thread some of the grapes onto a sturdy sprig of rosemary. And because there's got to be some wizardry on Halloween, garnish this drink with a flaming cinnamon stick before extinguishing it in the sangria to add a uniquely smoky flavor.

Décor Inspo
GOTHIC CHIC

When it comes to Halloween decorations, there are so many ways to go—from cheerful and kid-friendly pumpkins to downright gruesome ghouls. Victorian gothic lies somewhere in the middle, just enough creep with a dash of kitsch. Paper doilies or black lace make a maudlin backdrop for a collection of standard Halloween fare like faux ravens and plastic spiders, who've made themselves at home on a raw-edged board and a piece of moss-covered bark I found in the yard. Dim the lamps and light plenty of candles to set the mood.

A Modern Relish Tray

I LOVE THANKSGIVING for the same reason a lot of people do—it's family-focused without the pressure of exchanging gifts or attending services . . . not to mention, it's all about the food! For those in charge of hosting and cooking, however, it can be stressful. Lucky for me, my sister and I split the duties. She does most of the cooking while, not surprisingly, I oversee the appetizers and make the table "look pretty."

Growing up, we'd watch our mom prepare for days, making all the usual suspects like homemade stuffing, green bean casserole, and her infamous twice-baked potato boats and apple pie (see page 141). I'll never forget the story about her best crust. Running out of time, she shamefully resorted to using refrigerated piecrust, a relatively new product at the time. She didn't tell anyone about her shortcut, but when my dad exclaimed, "Judy, you've outdone yourself—this is your best piecrust yet!" she smiled to herself, and never made another crust from scratch again. Another example of where my "keep it simple" mantra comes from.

When I was little, I helped where I could, and my favorite job was to slice the canned cranberry jelly. (I know there are haters, but try it on a turkey sandwich the next day and then tell me you don't love the canned stuff.) My other job was to put together the "relish tray."

A staple appetizer of the '70s, a relish tray often included brined and marinated veggies, but ours was little more than green onions, celery, and jumbo black olives—the kind we would stick on the ends of our fingers and eat them off one by one! The same tray was on the table year after year, meant to be a palate cleanser, but it rarely got touched. I wonder now if the only reason it was there every Thanksgiving was because my mom knew I took great pride in putting it together, taking time to arrange the three ingredients just so.

Today my girls still have the satisfaction of slicing the canned cranberry, but somewhere along the way we stopped our relish tray tradition. Instead, I've started a new one, creating an updated version that, when served along with a few light cheeses, creamy hummus, and crispy crackers, is a perfect light snack leading up to the big meal. Though you could opt to marinate a variety of veggies or even shrimp (see page 140), in a pinch I pick my favorites from the olive bar at my grocery store.

On the Board

PICKLED/MARINATED ITEMS: Pitted green olives, pitted kalamata olives, caprese salad, Peppadew peppers, marinated artichoke hearts, green beans, mushrooms, and shrimp

ADDITIONAL ITEMS: Crackers, hummus

Whether you make your own or buy prepared ingredients for your relish tray from the grocery store, there are multiple ways you can serve them. Pile them up on one big platter, or spoon into individual bowls or jars and then group them together on a seasonal placemat or board. Here, I've transferred the snacks into pretty jars and tucked them into a primitive antique tool caddy, making it easy to carry to the coffee table for grazing during the football game. I love using mason jars so there's one less thing to clean up on Thanksgiving—just pop the lids on to store in the refrigerator.

Food Styling Tip
DEHYDRATED ORANGES

This tip works great for any citrus fruit and is an adornment that is as nice to look at as it is to smell. It's best to pick seedless oranges with deep porous peels and slice them thinly and uniformly. If you have an air fryer or dehydrator, you can use that, but if not, place the slices in a single layer on a parchment-paper-lined cookie sheet. Cook slow and low (I do 175 degrees for about three to six hours, depending on how thick the slices are) until they are no longer tacky to the touch.

Drink Pairing

MY GO-TO WITH A TWIST

No matter the season, my usual cocktail is a vodka soda with lemon. In the summer, I might add a splash of lemonade and basil. And in the cooler months, cranberry and a squeeze of fresh orange make it festive. **Make it a mocktail:** There's no better way to level up club soda or sparkling water, in my opinion, than with a splash of cranberry juice for a bit of tart and a squeeze of orange for a bit of sweet. Add the dried orange garnish for a festive touch. **Garnish:** You can use a fresh slice of orange, but for a more intense citrusy taste, opt for the dried oranges you used for decorating. A sprig of rosemary adds more depth of flavor and just the right hint of wintery pine.

Décor Inspo
RUSTIC PLACE SETTINGS

If you haven't already noticed, I am a big fan of using what you have on hand to decorate. In this case, I've taken the same dried oranges three ways—to add color to the relish tray, as a cocktail garnish, and finally to create a special place setting. Since I was going for a rustic look, I used some twine from the junk draw to tie slices around seasonal cloth napkins, topped with a wooden nametag I found at the craft store. For a more refined tablescape, swap twine for an elegant ribbon and wood for a proper place card.

Everyday Boards for Fall

THE TRANSITION FROM LOOSE SUMMER SCHEDULES to the more regimented school-year calendar always leaves me struggling for ideas for snacks and weeknight dinners. Employ the tips and tricks of the Gathering Board concept to help pull together meals and treats that will please everyone in the family.

Caramel Apple Board

If there's one taste that encapsulates autumn, for me it's caramel apples. As kids, we would make them using Wrapples—those sheets of caramel you wrap around the apple then heat them to melt. I thought that was the most ingenious invention, but I've found an even easier way—no sticks required. Think of it like a plate of nachos, only with apple slices smothered in caramel, chocolate, and crunchy toppings. Set out a bowl of sliced apples (tip: spray or dip them in lemon-lime soda to keep them from browning) alongside bowls of melted caramel and chocolate (tip: to keep warm, use a miniature fondue pot or crock pot, or microwave when needed). Set out bowls of toppings so everyone can create their own fall treat.

On the Board

APPLES: Sliced

SAUCES: Melted caramel, melted chocolate (milk, dark, and/or white)

TOPPINGS: Candy corn, chocolate chips, chopped nuts, crumbled cookies and/or candy bars, M&M's, mini marshmallows, shredded coconut, toffee bits

Ramen Board

When you hear "ramen," does it take you back to college where you cooked the block of noodles and powdered flavoring in a hotpot in your dorm? Or does it conjure thoughts of a night out at an upscale Japanese noodle house, a trend that continues to rise in popularity? Think of this ramen board as the perfect combination of both—it's fast, easy, and economical (yes, I use the instant dried noodles) but also full of complex flavors that are sophisticated enough for a dinner party. Start with boiling several packages of noodles in a large pot (put the flavor packets on the board for people to add to their bowl to their liking), then drain the noodles into a large bowl. This not only avoids soggy ramen, but also allows guests to ladle their desired ratio of noodles and broth before choosing from an array of toppings set out on a board. Provide both chopsticks and spoons for slurping!

On the Board

COOKED RAMEN NOODLES: In or removed from broth

PROTEINS: Chicken and/or steak, sliced; soft-boiled eggs

VEGGIES: Basil, chopped; bean sprouts; cabbage, shredded; carrots, shredded; cilantro, chopped; green onion, chopped; nori (seaweed); shiitake mushrooms, sliced; spinach

FLAVORINGS: Ramen flavor packs; soy sauce; sriracha; sweet chili sauce, chili crisp, and/or chili oil; Tabasco

Walking Taco Board

If you've ever had a kid play on a sports team, you've likely volunteered at the concession stand. That's where I discovered the wonders of the walking taco—a convenient, portable, and economical way to feed a crowd. They're popping up at carnivals, festivals, and concerts, too, so I decided to try one at home. It starts with a snack-size bag of chips, typically Doritos or Fritos, that are crushed a bit then topped with seasoned ground beef or chicken and all the usual toppings right in the bag. Shake to distribute the ingredients, and you've got a fun twist on "taco Tuesday" or a great meal for a kids birthday party or block party.

On the Board

BAGS OF CHIPS: Snack-size

PREPARED TACO MEAT

CHEESES: Cheddar cheese, shredded; queso fresco, crumbled

TOPPINGS: Cilantro, chopped; guacamole and/or sliced avocado; green chilies, diced; hot sauce; jalapeños, sliced; lettuce, shredded; salsa; sour cream; tomato, diced

10 Tips and Tidbits for Flawless Entertaining

THERE ARE LOADS OF TIPS scattered among the pages of this book, but here's a list of seemingly insignificant but impactful lessons I've learned over the years:

Sticky Notes

- When you are preparing for a party, be sure to take inventory of your platters and serving pieces a few days ahead of time. Jot every one of your menu items—from nuts to desserts—on a sticky note and assign each to a specific bowl or platter. Match up each dish with the proper utensils, because the last thing you need is to be hunting down a slotted spoon or set of tongs while trying to greet guests. I go so far as to arrange the labeled platters on the table, making sure there's plenty of room for everything.

Glassware

- I'm far from highbrow, but I just don't like to drink wine or cocktails out of a plastic cup. Paper plates don't bother me, but there's something about real glassware that makes drinks taste better and the party feel elevated. Even if they are mismatched, set out a variety of glasses for guests to choose from and reuse through the night. If you are having a larger party, consider renting or borrowing glassware, but if that's not in the budget, serve their first drink in a glass but have plenty of plastic for later in the night when, let's face it, less people care, if they did at all.

Lighting and Seating

- There are two things that can kill a party vibe instantly and are my greatest party pet peeves—too much light and chairs set up around the

perimeter of a room. Unless you're holding a focus group or planning an intervention, there's no reason to encourage guests to sit in a circle under harsh overhead lights, staring at one another. Instead, create a welcoming atmosphere with ambient light and candles, and set furniture and chairs in groupings of two or four to encourage socializing. Even if it's the kind of party where you'll gather round the guest of honor, try to wait a bit before you set up seating for gift opening to allow your guests to mingle.

Tunes

- If you've ever been the first person to walk into a party, you know it can feel awkward. But if there's music playing it not only fills the silence, but also lets your guests know you're ready for them, that they are welcome. Just like lighting, music can set the tone for your party. Have fun with a curated playlist fit for the occasion, or choose some pleasant jazz or acoustic to play upon guests' arrival. Remember, it's called background music for a reason. Keep the volume down to start, and as the party gets louder, so can the music.

Signature Drink

- A signature drink kills a flock of birds with one stone. First, it cuts down on costs to serve beer, wine, and one special cocktail (or mocktail) rather than stocking a full bar with various spirits and mixers. Second, it makes a self-service bar much less complicated (and messy), especially if you premix the signature drink in a large pitcher or dispenser. And last but not least, a signature cocktail is the perfect place to have fun with a theme with a specific color, clever name, or the guest of honor's favorite libation.

Drink Calculator

- This is a tip I wished I'd learned earlier in my entertaining career when I'd be scrambling to run to the store for more wine or beer. Generally speaking, the average guest drinks two beverages during the first hour of the party and one per hour after that. So, if your party is going to last for about three hours, that's four drinks per person. If you want to get very specific, find an online calculator in which you can plug in how many average, below average, and heavy drinkers are coming, as well as the types of drinks you're serving. In the end, I always tend to err on the side of too much rather than too little, as I know leftovers will be put to good use.

Party Flow

- Unless your home is built for entertaining, you'll likely discover a few bottlenecks when hosting a larger party. Take notice of where people tend to gather—typically near the bar, around the food, and almost always in the kitchen. Do what you can to ameliorate any overcrowding by spreading out the main attractions. Break up the bar by putting beer outside and wine and cocktails indoors, for instance, or serve appetizers on the kitchen island and a dinner buffet on the dining room table. Be sure not to block any doors and pathways so guests have options for moving about.

Garbage

- This tip may not be sexy, but it is oh-so-necessary. Don't forget to offer guests a place to put their garbage. If this rather mundane detail is overlooked, you might find yourself answering "Where's the garbage?" all night, or, worse, following guests around picking up used napkins, paper plates, and drink stirrers. Instead, simply place small trash and recycling bins in plain sight, preferably near the bar and food. This will make for easier post-party cleanup, too.

Bathrooms

- Though it's become customary at weddings, adding a thoughtful touch to the home powder room is a sure sign of a seasoned host. In addition to having plenty of soap and guest towels, add a small flower arrangement and scented candle to the sink. And if you're going all out, offer a basket of mints, gum, and other items for freshening up.

Have Fun!

- Last, but certainly not least, the best advice for any host is to be a guest at your own party! This is central to my entertaining philosophy because if you aren't having fun, your guests probably aren't either. By being prepared, choosing a simple menu that doesn't tie you to the kitchen all night, allowing guests to help themselves to drinks, and creating a relaxing atmosphere, you can sit back and enjoy the fruits of your labor.

Wine Pairing

WINE, CHEESE, AND CHARCUTERIE is a classic combination, so it's a topic about which I get lots of questions. I also get asked what my ultimate pairing is, if I had to pick a favorite. And since I simply cannot choose one, I'll start with three:

- Parmesan + Prosciutto + Chianti

- Manchego + Chorizo + Rioja

- Brie + Genoa Salami + Champagne

Everyone's preferences and palates are different, but the trick to finding your own ultimate pairing is to have fun experimenting. Wine, cheese, and charcuterie have a range of flavors and textures, so there's a lot to consider. Here are some general guidelines to help you get started:

- Match light-bodied wines with light cheeses and charcuterie, and full-bodied wines with richer cheeses and meats.

- Look for like flavors in your pairing. For example, try a nutty cheese like Manchego or Gouda with a nutty wine like sherry.

- Consider how acidic the wine is. A high-acid wine like a Riesling or pinot noir can cut through the richness of a higher-fat cheese or charcuterie better than a low-acid wine like merlot, which is a better fit with a milder cheese or charcuterie.

Four Classic Wine and Cheese Pairings to Try

- Sauvignon Blanc + Goat Cheese: The tangy flavors of goat cheese pair well with the citrusy flavors of sauvignon blanc.

- Champagne + Brie: The Brie's buttery texture and mild flavor pair well with the champagne's delicate bubbles and fruity notes.

- Pinot Noir + Gruyère: Earthy Gruyère complements the light, fruity flavors of pinot noir.

- Cabernet Sauvignon + Cheddar: Bold and fruity, cabernet sauvignon stands up to cheddar's sharp and tangy flavor.

Four Classic Wine and Charcuterie Pairings to Try

- Rosé + Prosciutto: The savory and salty flavors of prosciutto go well with rosé.

- Rioja + Chorizo: The Spanish sausage pairs best with fresh Spanish red wines like rioja.

- Zinfandel + Spicy Salami: The bold, spicy flavors of salami pair well with the rich, fruity flavors of zinfandel.

- Riesling + Capocollo: Riesling pairs well with meats like capocollo that have sweet, spicy flavor profiles.

How to Host a Wine-Cheese-Charcuterie Tasting Party

Hosting a wine-cheese-charcuterie party can be a great way to gather with friends. Suitable for any adult occasion, it is a nice way to get guests to mix and mingle, as it provides plenty of opportunities for conversation. There are countless ways to host a tasting party, none of which needs to be extravagant or complex. Here are some ideas:

- **Keep it casual.** A tasting party can come together within hours and requires only one or two stops. You can find good-quality wine, cheese, and meat, plus grab a bunch of flowers for the table, at just about any grocery store these days.

- **Stick to a few meats and a few cheeses.** Use the information in the "Board Basics" section to help guide you in selecting three of four of each. Don't go overboard, as it overcomplicates the pairings.

- **Choose affordable wines.** Settle on about four different wines, two white and two red. Stick with basic and easy-to-find varietals, nothing exotic or overly expensive. I stay in the $12 to $15 range.

- **Label your offerings.** I'm not typically a fan of labeling ingredients on my boards (I think it discourages people from trying new things), but in this case you want to help guests determine which pairings they like best.

- **Take notes.** Place a jar of pens and some sheets of paper on the table so people can jot down their favorites.

- **Guide your guests.** Using the information about pairings above, set up tasting stations. Each could have one wine, a cheese, and a charcuterie meat, along with some nuts, jam, or fruit.

- **Encourage experimentation.** Once guests have tasted their way through your pairing stations, invite them to mix and match to find their own.

EZPZ Recipes

MY FAVORITE KIND OF ENTERTAINING does not necessitate cooking. If you haven't concluded already, I am a master at avoiding complicated menus and recipes. I have, however, mentioned a few things in the Gathering Board repertoire that are far from complicated, but require a little bit more explanation. Here are a few of my go-to dips, meals, and sides:

Holiday Brie

SERVES 4–6

This four-ingredient appetizer is one that people drool over year after year. Sweet, salty, crunchy, creamy—need I say more? (Except to mention that it's also great the next day . . . just heat it up in the microwave.)

INGREDIENTS

- 1 8-ounce round Brie
- 1 cup light brown sugar
- ½ cup salted butter
- ½ cup sliced almonds

Leaving the Brie in its rind, set it out for about an hour to bring to room temperature (or microwave it for a minute or two, until slightly soft).

Place the sugar and butter in a saucepan over low heat and stir constantly until melted. Add the almonds and stir a minute or two to soften.

Place the softened Brie on a platter and pour the hot sugar mixture over it. Serve warm with a sliced baguette or water crackers.

Classic Swiss Fondue

SERVES 4–6

I often buy the premade vacuum-packed versions you can find in the cheese section of your grocery store. But making your own is an easy way to wow your guests and isn't nearly as difficult as you may think.

INGREDIENTS

- 1 pound Swiss cheese (I like a combination of Gruyère, Emmental, and Appenzeller)
- 2 tablespoons cornstarch
- 1 clove garlic, peeled and halved
- ½ cup dry white wine
- ½ teaspoon ground nutmeg
- 1 tablespoon kirsch (cherry liqueur) or brandy

FOR DIPPING:

- Fingerling potatoes, boiled
- Crusty bread, cubed
- Apples, sliced
- Cornichons

Shred the cheese into a large bowl, then stir in the cornstarch to coat the cheese. Rub the sides and bottom of a saucepan with garlic, then simmer both garlic halves and the white wine until hot.

Add the shredded cheese gradually to the wine, stirring constantly with a wooden spoon.

When the cheese has thoroughly melted, remove the garlic, add the nutmeg and kirsch, and stir. Pour into a fondue pot or chaffing dish and start dipping!

Simple Swiss Asparagus

SERVES 4–6

Zug, the small town where I lived in Switzerland, had some of the best restaurants. These were the type of places that locals loved, that rarely had fondue or raclette on the menu. Dishes weren't fancy, and there was something special about the humble way they served seafood. Freshly caught from a nearby lake, perch in butter or pike in lemon-cream sauce were among my favorites. During asparagus season, known as *Spargelzeit*, fish would always be accompanied by some version of simple, tender asparagus. This is the closest I've come to re-creating the classic Swiss *spargel*, which I also like to serve with ham or shrimp. If white isn't available, thick green asparagus will do. (Note: Unlike green, white asparagus is tough and must be trimmed. Use a vegetable peeler to remove the outer layer just below the tip all the way to the bottom, and cut off the woody ends.)

INGREDIENTS

- 1 teaspoon salt
- ¼ cup lemon juice
- 3 tablespoons butter
- 3 tablespoons sugar
- 1 pound white asparagus, trimmed

Fill a saucepan halfway with water and bring to a boil with the salt, lemon juice, butter, and sugar. Place the asparagus in the pan, reduce heat, and simmer 8 to 10 minutes or until tender.

Remove the asparagus from the pan and drain. Serve immediately.

Mom's Dill Dip

MAKES 1 CUP

I can't remember the last time, if ever, I made this dip using measurements. After so many years, I just toss the ingredients together and it always seems to work. But here's a start. Give it a test and then add more dill, onion, or seasoning mix to your taste.

INGREDIENTS

- ½ sour cream
- ½ cup mayonnaise
- 1 tablespoon dried onion
- 1 tablespoon dried dillweed
- 1 teaspoon Beau Monde seasoning

Mix all the ingredients together and refrigerate for at least an hour before serving to allow the onions to soften and flavors to mix. Serve with veggies for dipping, or on top of roasted salmon for a refreshing sauce.

Herbed Goat Cheese

SERVES 4–6

Goat cheese is one of those things that can be combined with just about anything, both sweet and savory. It's great with honey, fruit, and in the spring, fresh herbs. Many brands offer a variety of flavored goat cheese logs, including herbed. But here's a quick and easy recipe using fresh rather than dried herbs, along with some nuts for crunch. The result not only looks but also tastes like spring and is a great alternative to coating goat cheese in edible flowers, as shown in the Mother's Day Brunch Basket section.

INGREDIENTS

- 1 tablespoon finely chopped fresh parsley
- 1 tablespoon finely chopped fresh chives
- 1 tablespoon finely chopped fresh basil leaves
- 1 teaspoon lemon zest
- 1 clove garlic, minced
- 1 8-ounce goat cheese
- ½ cup chopped pecans

Combine the herbs in a bowl. Set aside 1½ teaspoons of the mixture for coating later. Add the lemon zest, garlic, and goat cheese to the bowl and mix to combine.

Form the cheese mixture into the shape of a log. Wrap in plastic and chill in the refrigerator for at least 30 minutes.

Mix the pecans and remaining herbs in a bowl, then spread on a plate or parchment paper. When the goat cheese is chilled, roll it in the mixture to coat it evenly. Serve with crackers, bread, or veggies.

Prepared Foods Counter Salmon Niçoise Salad

SERVES 4–6

This is my go-to dinner for gatherings requiring more food than an appetizer. It comes together super fast with help from my grocery store's prepared foods counter. I select not only a few pieces of roasted salmon, but also any kind of cooked beans and roasted potatoes from the display case. If prepared beans or potatoes aren't available, I simply boil them until soft and add some salt and pepper to taste.

INGREDIENTS

- 3 pounds roasted, grilled, or poached salmon
- 8 oz. bag chopped and cleaned lettuce
- 1 pound boiled or roasted fingerling or new potatoes
- ½ pound sautéed or steamed green beans
- 6 hard-boiled eggs, halved
- ½ cup Niçoise olives

FOR THE DRESSING:

- 1 lemon, juiced
- ¼ cup red wine or champagne vinegar
- ⅓ cup extra-virgin olive oil
- 1 tablespoon minced shallot
- 1 clove garlic, minced
- 2 tablespoons Dijon mustard
- 2 tablespoons capers
- ¼ teaspoon dried thyme
- 1 teaspoon salt
- 1 teaspoon freshly ground black pepper

For the dressing, place all the ingredients in a jar and shake vigorously until combined.

Plate the cooked fish over a bed of lettuce on a large platter. Pile the potatoes, green beans, eggs, and olives on the platter. Serve family style with the dressing on the side.

Tzatziki

MAKES 2 CUPS

This sauce is as common in Greece as ketchup is in the United States and is one of my favorite condiments. I eat it with just about everything, from sliced cucumbers and pita bread to fried dishes like zucchini and falafel. It can be found premade at the store but it's easy enough to whip up with ingredients you might already have in the fridge.

INGREDIENTS

- 1 large cucumber
- 1½ teaspoons salt, divided
- 2 cups plain Greek yogurt
- 2 tablespoons lemon juice
- 2 cloves garlic, minced
- 1 tablespoon chopped fresh dill

Cut the cucumber in half lengthwise and remove the seeds. Using a box grater, grate the cucumber and then place the pulp in a strainer and sprinkle with ½ teaspoon salt, allowing moisture to drain for about 15 minutes.

Squeeze the cucumber with your hands to remove excess liquid, then mix with the remaining ingredients. Serve cold or at room temperature.

Chautauqua Salad

SERVES 2–4

This salad is a key component of our family's favorite summer meal, "corn and tomatoes." It's nothing more than this simple cucumber and tomato dish served alongside corn on the cob and a crusty loaf of bread, a staple on nights when it's too hot for the oven or grill. We are lucky that our place on Chautauqua Lake is surrounded by corn fields and vegetable farms that supply our local roadside stand with the freshest ingredients for this simple summer supper.

INGREDIENTS

- ½ cup granulated sugar
- ¾ cup red wine vinegar
- ¼ cup extra-virgin olive oil
- 1 large cucumber, peeled and thinly sliced
- 2 large tomatoes, sliced

In a shallow bowl, dissolve the sugar in the red wine vinegar, then whisk in the oil. Gently fold in the tomatoes and cucumbers and allow to sit, at room temp, for at least 20 minutes.

Chilled Marinated Shrimp

SERVES 8–10

Instead of shrimp cocktail, try serving this dish as a light appetizer before a big meal. It comes together quickly and can made ahead of time and stored in the refrigerator for up to three days, making it especially convenient around the holidays. It's also great for an easy summer appetizer, a light salad over a bed of lettuce, or served hot over rice.

INGREDIENTS

- 3 tablespoons minced garlic
- 2 tablespoons olive oil
- ¼ cup lemon juice
- ¼ cup parsley, finely chopped
- ½ teaspoon salt
- ½ teaspoon pepper
- 1 tablespoon lemon zest
- 1 pound shrimp, cooked and peeled

Sauté the garlic in olive oil in a skillet over medium heat for about 1 minute, until fragrant. Add the lemon juice, parsley, salt, pepper, and lemon zest and toss the marinade with the shrimp in a large bowl. Chill until ready to serve.

Judy's Daughter's Apple Pie

MAKES 1 PIE

This was one of the first desserts my mom taught me and is the extent of my baking to this day. She and I made it together so many times, but I've decided to claim it as my own. I used to help her prep by peeling pounds of apples by hand until we discovered the Dazey Stripper, an electronic fruit and vegetable peeler. This time-saving invention, combined with my dad's stamp of approval on prepared piecrusts, shortened the process so much that as a teen, I felt confident enough to make it by myself, and I can't think of a fall since that I haven't made at least one. The hardest part has always been the crumble, which takes patience and some muscle to get it to the right consistency. But it's worth it, especially served warm with a scoop of vanilla ice cream.

INGREDIENTS

- 1 cup brown sugar, divided
- 1 cup flour, sifted
- ¾ cup butter, cold and sliced into pads or cubes
- 6 cups cored, peeled, and sliced apples
- ¼ teaspoon cinnamon
- 1 refrigerated piecrust

For the crumble, combine ½ cup of the brown sugar and the flour in a mixing bowl. Add butter chunks and incorporate using a pastry cutter or a pair of butter knives cutting in a crisscross motion. This can take some time but be sure to stop once you've reached a course crumble, as you don't want to overmix into a dry dough consistency. My mom often used a food processor to pulse the three ingredients together, though I prefer hand mixing. Chill in the refrigerator until ready to use.

For the filling, combine the apples, ½ cup of the brown sugar, and the cinnamon. Following the directions on the box, unroll the pie dough, and press it into a pie pan. Pour the apple mixture into the piecrust and top with the crumble. Bake uncovered at 425 degrees for 45 to 50 minutes. If the crumble gets too brown, cover for the last 15 minutes.

Acknowledgments

THERE ARE SO MANY PEOPLE FOR WHOM I AM INCREDIBLY GRATEFUL for their love and support before, during, and after this book went from a pipe dream to reality.

To friends and neighbors who believed in this, long before I believed in myself, whether it was brainstorming, taste-testing cheese, or folding hundreds of salami slices for big orders. To my first customers and collaborators who got EZPZ Gatherings off the ground in the midst of a global pandemic, and to mentors who guided me in those early days.

I am profoundly grateful for Michael Lyons at Rowman & Littlefield, whose email popped up in May of 2022 with subject line "Charcuterie Article and Book Idea" and made me stop dead in my tracks. And to Michael's mother for passing along a little article to him about my business, a simple act that was nothing short of life-changing. Thank you to Judith Schnell and the team at Globe Pequot, whose guidance and patience for this first-time author was both comforting and edifying.

A shout-out to two special cohorts and cohosts in life: my friend Andi, with whom I developed a love of food and for throwing holiday parties, which, for a couple single girls in our twenties, were rather extravagant; and Amanda, my friend and partner in crime for just about anything from chairing elaborate fund-raisers and events to rearranging furniture and raising kids.

And thanks to Kari, my friend and photographer who made this book not just gorgeous, but so much fun. As they say, we make a good team.

To my family. My niece, Alison, for her stellar graphic design skills and nephew, Duncan, who I could always count on to polish off leftovers. Of course, a huge thank-you to my dad, Scott, without whom I would lack both time and resources, and to Martha—my best friend, sissy, and unpaid employee—without whom I would lack the strength (mental and physical) required for this endeavor. To my mom, Judy, who sparked my joy of gathering friends and family with the promise of good food, lots of wine, and even more laughter. I miss you every day but here I am, out walking in a crystal blue morning, lettin' life carry on.

And finally, I'd like to recognize my remarkable daughters, Lydia and Edie, for their steadfast support and praise. Every "You got this, mom" text or "I'm so proud of you" hug means more than you know. My hope is I've shown you that it's never too late to dream a new dream.

About the Author

GATHERING BOARDS IS THE DEBUT BOOK of Sarah Zimmerman Tuthill, freelance writer and owner of EZPZ Gatherings, LLC. Born and raised in Pittsburgh, Pennsylvania, her career as a communications professional took her to Atlanta then Switzerland, where she developed a passion for food, traveling, entertaining, and interior design. Settling back in her hometown, she is a contributing writer for local lifestyle magazines that focus on such topics. The author has been featured in both national and regional publications and is a regular guest on local television talk shows.

Sarah launched EZPZ Gatherings in 2019 as a way of bringing her passions together, creating made-to-order cheese and charcuterie boards for parties, weddings, and events. The storefront serves as prep space for fulfilling orders and is where the author hosts "Boarding School" workshops in which she's taught over one thousand students about cheese and charcuterie styling.

The storefront is located in Aspinwall, a bustling small town just east of Pittsburgh, where she lives, just two short blocks from her shop, with two teenaged daughters and their beloved yellow Lab.